PRESSURE COOKING

the MEATLESS WAY

Over 125 Delicious and Nutritious Recipes for Today's Busy Cook

MAUREEN B. KEANE
DANIELLA CHACE

Prima Publishing

PRIMA PUBLISHING and colophon are trademarks of Prima Communications, Inc.

Illustrations by Daniella Chace

Library of Congress Cataloging-in-Publication Data

Keane, Maureen.
 Pressure cooking the meatless way : over 125 delicious and nutritious recipes for today's busy cook / by Maureen B. Keane and Daniella Chace.
   p. cm.
  Includes index.
  ISBN 0-7615-0032-4
  1. Pressure cookery. 2. Vegetarian cookery.   I. Chace, Daniella.   II. Title.
TX840.P7K39   1996
641.5'87—dc20   95-48043
                                                                                            CIP

96 97 98 99 00 AA 10 9 8 7 6 5 4 3 2 1
Printed in the United States of America

HOW TO ORDER

Single copies may be ordered from Prima Publishing, P.O. Box 1260BK, Rocklin, CA 95677; telephone (916) 632-4400. Quantity discounts are also available. On your letterhead, include information concerning the intended use of the books and the number of books you wish to purchase.

We would like to dedicate this book to Buck Levin, Ph.D., R.D., a wonderful teacher who has given us much insight into the science and art of nutrition.

Contents

Preface

It's time for me to come out of the kitchen closet. I don't mean to shock anyone, but I hate to cook. I hate all the chopping, slicing, and dicing, I hate the watching and stirring, the boiling and the simmering, and finally I hate all the dirty bowls, oily skillets, and burned pots the process produces. The only redeemable feature of cooking is that it produces (usually) edible, tasty food that quiets the rumbling hunger in my belly. That is why the four cookbooks Dani and I have written for Prima Publishing stress convenience, ease of use, and simplicity.

Of all the new-fangled inventions and appliances in my kitchen, the most used is my pressure cooker. With two of us working and three of us eating in my family, the pressure cooker is sometimes the only way I can get dinner on the table. It makes healthy food, fast food.

When I cook beans, I rarely presoak. They are just thrown into the pressure cooker and splashed with an estimated amount of water. I prefer to pressure steam the grains; they remain much more fluffy and separate. And if anything is underdone, I just add a tad more water and bring to pressure again.

What goes into dinner is what happens to be in the pantry or fridge. Our recipes reflect this, and are designed to be flexible and foolproof for the impatient ad-lib cook.

I hope you enjoy this book and the pleasure of pressure cooking.

MAUREEN KEANE

Once you get into the rhythm of using a pressure cooker, you may find your other pots and pans stay shining and hanging from their rack and become solely decorative.

I use my pressure cooker as a sauté pan, soup pan, casserole dish, and vegetable steamer. Many of the recipes I have developed start with sautéing onions, then adding the remaining ingredients and cooking everything all in one pot. You will pick up "quick tricks" like cooking your grains in the pressure cooker, setting them aside, then throwing in whatever vegetables are in the fridge or in the garden and steaming them with a light dressing. Spooned over the grains they make a complete, nutritious meal.

Healthy foods that Americans are not eating enough of include legumes (beans, peas, and lentils); whole grains like quinoa, barley, and brown rice; and fresh fruits and vegetables. I have heard countless stories from clients who want to eat more beans but they feel they take too long to cook and they don't know what to do with them once they are cooked!

This is where the pressure cooker works magic in the kitchen. Rather than the usual hours of prep time, the average total preparation time for dried bean recipes using the pressure cooker is only twenty minutes. Grains are just as easy and quick in the pressure cooker. They become infused with flavors that need little dressing up. Cooked in vegetable broth and scented with just a few favorite herbs, your grains will be full of flavor and plump with moisture.

Your pressure cooker will quickly become your favorite tool for making fast gourmet cuisine. Enjoy!

DANIELLA CHACE

Acknowledgments

$\mathcal{A}$ big thank you to the following individuals who provided pressure cookers and literature for our research: Fraser Laurie of Bo/Nash, Lydia Hawryluk and Virginia Kiremidjian of Faberware, Patricio Barriga of Fagor America, Jack Knipple of Hawkins Futura, Phil Ryan of Innovations, Joann O'Gara of National Presto Industries, Lonnie and Peter Bumann of Susamat, Rosey Pulaski of Wearever-Mirro, and Philip Jacobs of the Wisconsin Aluminum Foundry Company.

Thank you to our helpers and panel of recipe judges: John Keane, Tara Hubbard, Nels Moulton, Eric Moulton, Thad Nicolai, Brad Torres, Merrilee Gomez, Nuria Gomez, Jake Koch, Dylan Koch, Rusty Dill, E. J. Moulton, Carol Moulton, and of course our expert taste-tester, Woo Moulton.

Special appreciation to the amateur physicist Natalie Koch for her descriptions of pressure cooking engineering and technical advice.

PRESSURE COOKING
the MEATLESS WAY

part

I

YOUR

PRESSURE

COOKER

A startling variety of cooking appliances and machines is at the disposal of today's cook. Once purchased, these tools are used religiously for a few weeks. After the novelty wears off, they are retired to the appliance garage for guest appearances, eventually being laid to rest in the dust of the lower shelf.

Except for the pressure cooker. This kitchen workhorse is destined to become your most frequently used appliance. It does what the microwave cannot: cook beans and whole grains with astonishing speed. For meatless cooking it has no rival. Even the cheapest, most basic models are sturdy and easy to use. Properly cared for, your pressure cooker may outlive you and pass to another generation of needy cooks.

Part I of this book is a primer on pressure cooking. It will explain the theory behind pressure cooking, aid in troubleshooting, and detail how to use and care for your cooker. Read this part first to avoid making common mistakes.

1

PARTS
AND
MAINTENANCE

The principles of cooking with superheated steam in a sealed pot are almost three hundred years old. For more than seventy years, American manufacturers have been making and selling pressure pots for use in the home. Today's pressure cookers operate on the same principles as the original designs but with fewer problems. Simple mechanisms for pressure release and overpressure plugs have made the cookers safer, easier, and more convenient to use.

Cooking with pressure is faster than other methods of cooking for the simple reason that the temperature inside a sealed pan is hotter than the temperature inside an open pan. When heated in an open pan, water molecules absorb the heat applied by the heating element. This energizes the water molecules and eventually they absorb enough energy to fly into the air as steam. The temperature at which this occurs is called the boiling point.

Boiling points differ because the amount of energy needed to push through the air molecules differs from place to place. The higher you climb above sea level, the less dense the air. For example, there are fewer air molecules in a Denver kitchen than in a Seattle kitchen of the same size. This is because Denver is very high above sea level. It takes less energy for an energized water molecule to jump out of the pan in Denver than it does in Seattle. At sea level, where most of us live, the boiling point is 100 degrees Celsius or 212 degrees Fahrenheit. Water in an open pan cannot get above its boiling temperature because when it does it ceases to be water and becomes steam.

In a closed pan like the pressure cooker, the water molecules also absorb energy and escape into the air in the pan. Since the pan is closed, only a limited amount of space is available. Soon the air is packed with water molecules and there is no more room for steam. All the crowded steam molecules push down on the liquid. This push is called pressure. The energized molecules then have no choice but to remain as a liquid and keep absorbing heat. Now the temperature of the water starts to rise.

The pressure regulator, a weight on top of the vent pipe, allows air and then steam to escape when the pressure of the excited water molecules becomes too great. Most pressure gauges are set at 15 pounds of pressure. This means that the molecules in the water vapor are pushing on the water molecules in the liquid at 15 pounds of pressure. If the heat continues to rise, the pressure at which the water vapor is pushing down on the water molecules in the liquid increases and lifts the weight slightly off the vent pipe, allowing steam to escape into the air, thereby equalizing the pressure.

ADVANTAGES OF PRESSURE COOKING

Most cooks are attracted to the pressure cooker by its convenience. Pressure cooking is quicker than cooking on a regular stovetop or oven and in some cases even quicker than the microwave oven. This makes it a must for two-career families and busy parents. And once high pressure is reached, the food does not have to be stirred, turned, or otherwise tended. Just set the timer, relax, and return to the kitchen when it goes off. The time savings are actually very dramatic. Pressure cookers are at least three times faster than normal cooking methods and are about twice as fast as the microwave oven.

Pressure cooking is ideal for people who are concerned about nutrition. Foods prepared in the pressure cooker retain more of their vitamins than foods cooked by other means. The destruction of fat-soluble vitamins by oxygen is reduced because the steam drives most of the oxygen out of the sealed pan. In an open pan, water-soluble vitamins can be lost to the steam or cooking water. This does not happen in the pressure cooker where less water is used and little steam is allowed to escape. Food comes out tasting light and is heart-healthy.

Most cooking odors are trapped in the pressure cooker, leaving them in the pot and not in your kitchen. For example, the odors of cabbage and other sulfur-containing vegetables are kept to a minimum. This also means that the flavors are not lost to the air.

Once the cooker reaches high pressure, only a small amount of heat is needed to keep the pot at that pressure. This produces less heat in the kitchen, making it a necessity for hot-weather cooking.

The pressure cooker is also a "green" appliance. It uses less water and fuel, both nonrenewable natural resources, than other cooking methods. Its small size makes it perfect for camping trips, for use in recreational vehicles, or for a dorm room.

And last but not least, the cooker is versatile. You can make a whole meal or a single entrée, everything from hearty stews to delicate custards. Precooking such as browning and steaming can be done in the cooker. After cooking, ingredients can be added or the dish can be thickened.

PARTS OF THE PRESSURE COOKER

The pressure cooker comes in a wide variety of styles and models but the basic principals are the same behind each one. The outside of the cooker is usually aluminum. The inside is sometimes coated with a nonstick surface. A trivet or steam basket of some kind is always included for steaming foods. Cooker shapes and sizes vary greatly from large, tall, and potlike to the short, flat skillet type.

Built into the lid is a pressure regulator. Often this is a weight that fits over the vent pipe. A cover or vent lock allows air in the cooker to escape and seals off to prevent steam from escaping. A gasket or sealing ring fits around the inner edge of the lid. Its purpose is to form a tight pressure seal between the lid and the pot. An overpressure plug will pop off to release steam if the pressure rises too high. Pressure cookers rarely get broken in the course of daily use. Problems usually arise from a lack of maintenance, and can be easily prevented or fixed.

THE OVERPRESSURE PLUG

The overpressure plug is a safety mechanism that allows pressure to escape in case the vent pipe becomes blocked. Over time and with use, this pliable rubber plug may become hard and inflexible. This prevents it from working as a pressure release valve and it should be replaced immediately.

If the plug blows out, a blocked vent pipe has caused the pressure inside of the cooker to exceed safety limits. Immediately cool the cooker if this happens. When the cooker is completely cooled, remove the lid and clean the vent pipe with a piece of wire or a bent paper clip under running water. Once a plug has been blown out of the lid, it has served its purpose and cannot be used effectively again. Consult your owner's manual about how to purchase a replacement.

GASKETS

The gasket forms the seal between the lid and the body of the pressure cooker. This smooth pliable ring takes a lot of wear and tear and should be replaced periodically. See your manufacturer's recommendations about when to replace the gasket. The sealing gasket should be cleaned frequently.

The gasket needs to be replaced when: it becomes hard and brittle or soft and sticky; steam escapes around the rim of the cooker when the vent pipe is clear and open; the gasket has shrunk; or the gasket becomes loose and stretched.

COOKER MAINTENANCE

Treat the outside of your cooker like any fine piece of aluminum cookware. Use a nonabrasive cleaner and sponge to remove burned-on food. Occasionally clean the exterior with a fine silver polish to renew its luster. Avoid the use of harsh scouring pads and abrasive cleaners that could dull the exterior.

The interior of your cooker cleans up so easily you should only need a mild soap solution and a sponge. To preserve the lining, avoid using metal utensils, harsh scouring pads, and abrasive cleaners, which can make fine scratches and discolor the surface.

If you burn food to the bottom of the open pan, pour about $^{1}/_{2}$ cup of baking soda and about 1 inch of water into the open pan and boil it for a few minutes. All the burned food just comes off. Use a scrub sponge or a brush to wipe out the bottom and it's clean.

Aluminum cookers can be discolored by iron and other minerals in the water and food. To remove these stains, add water to the cooker and 1 tablespoon of cream of tartar for each quart of water. Make sure the solution covers the discoloration. Cover the cooker, bring to high pressure, remove from heat, and let sit for 2 to 3 hours. Empty cooker, scour it with a safe plastic pad, wash, rinse, and dry. An alternative method is to boil one part vinegar to one part water in the *open* cooker, then wash, rinse, and dry.

Overheating the cooker can also cause varicolored stains called heat tints. These can be removed by using a copper or stainless steel cleaner.

These are just general instructions. Refer to your owner's manual before you begin to use your cooker. Properly maintained, it will give you years of service and enjoyment.

2

TIPS
AND
TRICKS

Not all pressure cooking proceeds smoothly. Luckily, most problems can be quickly solved or easily prevented. These tips will help to keep you pressure cooking at full steam.

STEAM LEAKAGE

Do not be concerned if you notice a leakage of small amounts of steam or water around the lid and handles. This is normal when cooking first starts. If steam continues to escape or pressure does not rise, it means that a seal has not formed between the lid and the pan.

Remove the pan from the heat source and when the cooker is cool to the touch, remove the lid. Inspect the vent pipe, making sure that it is clean and not clogged by food particles. Check that the gasket is in good condition and has not shrunk.

Check the rim of the pan. If the rim is dented from banging spoons and other wear and tear on the cooker, the gasket may not be able to form a seal. If the lift pin and gasket are in good working order, realign the handles, making sure they fit properly, and then start over.

STICKING LID

If you cannot get the cooker to open after cooking is complete, it may be the pressure is not fully down. A clogged vent tube may be preventing pressure release. After cooker has cooled, clean vent pipe with a wire.

The gasket in the lid could be stuck to the rim of the cooker. This is the result of food bubbling up around the lid. To avoid this in the future, do not fill your cooker more than two-thirds full. If liquids continue to bubble up, decrease the cooker volume to half or bring the food to pressure on medium rather than high heat.

FOAMING AND CLOGGED VENT

Most manufacturers recommend against cooking applesauce, cranberries, rhubarb, split peas, pearl barley, oatmeal, soup mixes containing dried vegetables, or other cereals and pastas including macaroni and spaghetti. These foods are likely to foam during cooking and clog the vent pipe.

That said, we have successfully cooked smaller amounts of applesauce, cranberries, split peas, pearl barley, and oatmeal, by pressure steaming them in a separate bowl. Pressure steaming instructions can be found in chapter 3.

PRECISION TIMING

To get the best job out of your cooker, you will need to have a timer. A wide variety of timers are available at specialty stores to fit both your pocketbook and your tastes. For precision timing:

1. Set your timer as soon as the pressure regulator begins to turn, hiss, or rock.
2. Reduce the heat until the pressure regulator turns, hisses, or rocks slowly. This means that the regulator turns or rocks 1 to 4 times a minute. Any faster than that and you are wasting energy and losing steam.
3. Remove the cooker from the heat source as soon as the timer goes off.
4. If timing must be precise (with vegetables, for example) or if testing for doneness, quickly cool under cold running water.
5. Wait until the pressure regulator stops moving and hissing and the vent lock falls. Never attempt to open your cooker until all pressure has been released.
6. Now it is safe to open your cooker. If needed, the cooker can be resealed and brought again to high pressure for more cooking.

OVERCOOKING

Given the speed with which pressure pans cook, overcooking is not uncommon in the beginning. If a food is too mushy to serve, save it for a soup or stew. Some burned-on foods give a lovely smoky flavor to recipes.

To prevent this overcooking, always use a timer to accurately measure cooking time. In addition:

- Use the largest burner on your range so that heat is distributed evenly over the bottom of the cooker.
- Cover the entire bottom of the cooker with water. At least a half cup is necessary for most pot and saucepan-type cookers, but you should follow the recommendations of your manufacturer.
- Use a medium to high heat setting to raise cooker to high pressure. Too low a temperature can cause the food to burn before reaching the proper pressure.
- Use low heat setting after cooker reaches pressure. Too high a flame will cause the steam to burn away.
- Before adding the food, coat the bottom of the cooker with a nonstick spray or lightly coat the bottom with oil.
- Thick mixtures, like chili and tomato sauces, burn easily. Thin them by adding water. After cooking the food can be thickened again by reducing the mixture with the cover off or by adding a thickening agent such as cornstarch, arrowroot, or flour.

LIQUID FOR COOKING

The pressure cooker needs a certain amount of liquid to generate the pressure. This amount varies from cooker to cooker and manufacturer to manufacturer. In general, skillet-type pressure cookers need the least amount of water and the large, pot-type cookers need more. Always read the directions that came with your cooker and follow the manufacturer's instructions.

The need for water can be satisfied by other liquids that consist mostly of water, including canned broth, bottled cooking sauces, diluted canned soups, wine, beer, stocks, tomato and other vegetable juice, cider, and fruit juice.

PRESSURE COOKER DO'S

Do reduce pressure before removing the cover.

Do read your instruction manual and follow your manufacturer's instructions.

Do use only ovenproof casseroles and dishes inside of the cooker. If plastic containers are not dishwasher safe, they are not pressure cooker safe.

Do be creative with cooking liquids. Wine, beer, porter, canned stocks, ciders, and juices all make wonderful additions. Have fun and use your imagination.

Do use your cooker to dry-roast grains before pressure cooking. This will increase the flavor of the grains.

Do brown onions, garlic, leeks, scallions, and carrots before cooking to caramelize and increase the depth of flavor.

Do thicken cooking liquid for use as a gravy or sauce. Just add 1 teaspoon of arrowroot, cornstarch, or flour for every 1 cup of liquid. Heat with cover off and stir until thickened.

Do keep your hand away from the steam if your cooker has a steam release valve. Hot steam can cause painful burns.

PRESSURE COOKER DON'TS

Don't remove the cover until you are sure pressure has fallen.

Don't try to fry foods under pressure. The oil will not produce steam and will eventually catch fire.

Don't cook pasta. Pasta needs time to rehydrate and pressure cooking will not speed up the process.

Don't fill the cooker over half full when making stews and soups. This will prevent the liquids from boiling up and clogging the vent.

Don't add viscous ingredients such as tomato paste straight to the cooker; always thin them down with water first. Thick ingredients will stick to the bottom of the pan and burn.

Don't be afraid to experiment with your pressure cooker. Some of the best soups and stews our families ate came from overcooking recipes we were developing.

Oils are not suitable as a cooking liquid. When boiled they will not release steam and can cause a fire. This will also happen with oil-based marinades and dressings.

Milk, yogurt, sour cream, and other milk-based products should also be avoided. They have a tendency to boil over or foam, and could potentially clog the vent. Add milk products after cooking has finished.

You can never have too much water in a recipe. If the taste is too diluted, just simmer to evaporate the excess water. Thickeners can also be added after the cooker is opened.

part
II

RECIPES

The refrigerator may be empty, the freezer may be bare, the canned goods may be exhausted, but if you are a vegetarian, a hearty meal always awaits you in your pantry. It may take a few hours of soaking and slow cooking, but eventually a delicious, nutritious meal materializes. Unless you own a pressure cooker. Then you can indulge those taste buds in less than 30 minutes.

Vegetarians rely on the very foods that a pressure cooker is made to conquer. The pressurized steam brings to life dried grains, beans, and seeds, infusing them with all the flavors and fragrances of the herbs, spices, and vegetables that accompany them.

Remember, your finished meal is only as good as the ingredients that went into it. Use only the best produce, freshest grains, and the highest-quality spices you can afford.

3

BASIC
DISHES

Use this chapter for simple recipes and to create one-of-a-kind creations of your own.

HOW TO COOK ANYTHING

The most common method of pressure cooking is to place the food directly into the pan. By combining the solids and liquids, flavors can mingle during cooking. This is particularly important when making stews, soups, and casseroles, and for poaching fruits. The superheated steam shoots out the flavors and mingles them together as if they had been cooking all day.

To pressure cook your own original recipes, follow these simple steps:

1. Spray the inside of the pan with nonstick cooking spray or heat with olive or canola oil.
2. If you are going to brown any ingredients such as onions, garlic, leeks, or mushrooms, do it now.
3. Add all of the ingredients, including adequate liquid.
4. Place the lid on the cooker, seal, and turn the heat on high.
5. When the pressure regulator starts to rock, hiss, or spin, turn the heat down and set your timer for the recommended cooking time. The cooker is at appropriate low heat when the pressure regulator rocks slowly and steadily.
6. When the timer goes off, remove the cooker from heat. For recipes that contain large amounts of liquid, let the pressure fall on its own.
7. Take off the lid carefully and remove food. Remember hot steam can burn you.
8. The liquid remaining from poaching can now be thickened and used as a sauce, or frozen for later use as soup base.

HOW TO STEAM IT ALL

Your pressure cooker can also be used to pressure steam foods, using the trivet or basket that came with your cooker. Many different foods can be steamed in the pressure cooker at the same time without flavors mingling.

For pressure steaming foods cooked in containers, use only ovenproof glass or metal cups or boilable plastic bowls, and cook for an additional 4 to 6 minutes. Make sure that the highest point of the dish does not rise above the cooker's two-thirds mark.

To steam foods follow these steps:

1. Place the recommended amount of water into the pan.

Remember that the longer a food takes to cook, the more water it needs.

2. Coat the trivet or basket with nonstick vegetable spray or olive oil, and place it in the pot.

3. Place the food directly onto the trivet. Make sure that the water does not touch the food and that the food does not touch the sides of the cooker.

4. Place the lid on the cooker, seal it, and turn the heat on high. For recipes that contain all wine or for recipes with ingredients that have a tendency to foam, bring to high pressure on medium heat.

5. When the pressure regulator starts to rock, hiss, or spin, turn the heat down and set your timer for the recommended cooking time. The cooker is at appropriate low heat when the pressure regulator rocks slowly and steadily.

6. When the timer goes off, remove the cooker from heat. For quick-cooking recipes, particularly delicate vegetables, place the cooker under cold running water until the pressure regulator falls.

7. Take off the lid carefully and, using mitts or a fork, remove trivet with food.

HOW TO RELEASE PRESSURE

When food has cooked or steamed for the recommended amount of time, reduce the pressure before removing the lid. Pressure can be reduced in three ways:

Slow release method   This is the easiest but not the fastest. Simply let the cooker sit quietly until the pressure drops of its own accord. It is the recommended release method for soups, stews, and some delicate desserts.

Steam release button method   Some cookers have a quick steam release button. The pressure is reduced by letting the steam escape. When it is held down, the steam shoots out. Make sure no fingers are in the path of the steam since it can burn. This method takes anywhere from 15 to 30 seconds.

If your machine does not have a steam release button or for some reason you do not want odors from the cooker (for example, if you are cooking cauliflower or cabbage) circulating in the house, use the quick release method described below. The button method is not suitable for use with stews and soups or any recipe that fills the cooker almost to capacity. This is because the removal of the steam causes boiling food to bubble into the vent pipe and sputter or shoot hot liquid, often clogging the vent.

Quick release method   This method is the fastest, and safest: quick release under water. Simply carry the cooker over to the sink and run cold water on it. Keep a couple of oven mitts around to help with this and make sure the sink is empty. In just a few seconds the pressure inside will fall. Then when you open the cooker, no odors will escape and no dangerous steam will accost you.

Once you get used to working with your particular cooker you may find that combinations of these methods best suit your cooking style. For example, you may wish to let the cooker sit quietly for 5 minutes and then use the steam release button. Or you may wish to use the slow release method for a number of minutes and then quick release under water.

Some people are intimidated by pressure cookers because of the noise they make. There's no need for fear. Pressure cookers are one of the safest appliances you can have in your kitchen. Before long, your pressure cooker will be your best friend.

Steamed Grains

MAKES 2½ CUPS

The pressure cooker can steam grains much faster than rice cookers, the microwave, or a saucepan. The grains come out fluffy and separate, and cleanup is easier. The cooking dish can go from cooker to table.

1   cup grain of choice (see table)

Add ½ to 2 cups water to the empty cooker. The amount of water is determined by how long the grains need to cook. The longer the cooking time, the more water you need.

Place a trivet or rack inside the cooker.

Add uncooked grain to an ovenproof glass dish that fits easily inside of the cooker. We prefer those with glass lids. To calculate the amount of water to put into the grain-filled dish, add the number of cups of uncooked grain to the number of cups in the yield (see table). Add this much liquid.

Cover and place dish on top of the trivet inside the cooker. Fit lid on cooker, seal, and bring to high pressure quickly. Lower the heat quickly and set your timer for the recommended cooking time. Reduce pressure quickly under cold running water after the recommended amount of time.

TIPS FOR GRAINS

- Never fill the cooking dish over two-thirds full. The grains need room to expand.

COOKING TIMES

Grain (1 cup)	Minutes Cooking at High Pressure	Yield (cups)
amaranth	4	2
barley, unhulled	50–60	3
barley, pearled	17–20	3½
buckwheat/kasha°	0–1	2
cornmeal/polenta	5	5
kamut berries	30–35	2
millet	5–8	3
oats, groats°	25–30	2
quinoa°	5–6	2½
rice, brown, long	35	2
rice, brown, short	25	2½
rye berries	30–35	2
spelt	30–40	2
teff°	6–8	3
wheat, bulgur°	5	2½
wheat berries	35–40	2
wild rice°	25–30	3½

° Reduce pressure quickly under cold running water.

- If you prefer to cook grains directly in the cooker without a trivet and cooking dish, always add 1 tablespoon oil, and let the pressure fall on its own for 5 to 10 minutes before quick-cooling.
- Cooking times for grains can vary greatly, depending on factors such as the age of the grain, how dry it is, and storage conditions.
- Short grain brown rice takes longer to cook than long or medium grain.

Legumes

MAKES 2 TO 2½ CUPS

Beans should be rehydrated before they are cooked. This treatment prepares the beans for cooking and removes much of the gas-causing substances. There are two methods of rehydration.

For the overnight soak method wash beans and pick out any debris. Put 3 cups water to every 1 cup beans in a bowl and let sit overnight. Drain well, rinse, and use.

For the quick-soak method wash beans and pick out any debris. Place in pressure cooker with 3 cups water for every 1 cup beans. Seal cooker and bring to high pressure. Lower heat and cook for 5 minutes. Remove from heat and let pressure fall on its own. Drain well, rinse, and use.

1   cup legumes of choice (see table)

Add beans to unsalted water. Never fill the cooker more than one-third full and be sure the beans are covered with water. Add one tablespoon of oil per cup of beans to the cooking water (check your cooking instructions for the minimum amounts of cooking liquid), cover, and bring to pressure. Lower heat, cook for appropriate time (see table), and reduce heat with the quick release method.

TIPS FOR LEGUMES

• Store dried beans in tightly covered containers in a cool, dry place, and they will keep for months. Do not store in refrigerator.

COOKING TIMES

Legumes (1 cup)	Minutes Cooking at High Pressure
adzuki beans	2–3
black beans	5–8
black eyed peas °	10
cannellini beans	5–8
chickpeas (garbanzo beans)	10–13
cranberry beans	5–9
great northern beans	4–9
kidney beans	4–8
lentils°	4–6
lima beans	1–3
navy beans	3–5
pinto beans, pink or white	1–3
small white beans	10
soybeans	35
split peas °	6–10
whole peas	4–6

° Do not presoak.

Add a couple of bay leaves to each container; it is said they discourage insects and other unwanted creepy crawlies.

- Dried beans double in volume and in weight after soaking and cooking. Rule of thumb: 1 cup (8 ounces) dried beans equals 2 to 2½ cups (1 to 1¼ pounds) soaked and cooked beans.

- When buying canned beans, be sure to read labels. Look for organic beans and avoid those that list preservatives, additives, and animal fat.

- Soaked beans (both overnight- and quick-soaked) can be stored in the freezer for up to 2 months.

Vegetables

Recipes for vegetable side dishes can be found in chapter 6. Dress up plain vegetables with sauces found in chapter 4.

Vegetables of choice (see table)

Place vegetables into a trivet, bowl, or directly into pressure cooker. Add appropriate amount of water (see your cooker's manual). Bring up to high pressure quickly. Reduce temperature immediately and cook for the appropriate time (see table). Always cool cooker under cold running water.

Add 3 to 5 minutes to given cooking time when pressure steaming vegetables in a container. Add 1 to 4 minutes when steaming vegetables on a trivet.

TIPS FOR VEGETABLES

- If at all possible, buy and use only organic produce. If not, scrub all vegetables in warm soapy water to remove surface pesticides and trim off any damaged spots, edges, or leaves. Peel vegetables such as potatoes, beets, turnips, kohlrabi, and any vegetable that has been waxed.
- Large vegetables, such as squash, and head vegetables should be cut into smaller pieces before cooking. Remember, the time it takes food to cook in the pressure cooker depends on the size of the pieces, not the number of pieces.

FROZEN VEGETABLE COOKING TIMES

Vegetable	Minutes Cooking at High Pressure
asparagus	2
beans, green or wax	1
beans, lima	1
broccoli	2–4
brussels sprouts	2–2½
cauliflower florets	2–3
cauliflower, whole	6–8
corn on the cob	4–5
corn, kernels	3
mixed vegetables	2
peas	1
spinach	1

- Root vegetables such as white potatoes, sweet potatoes, yams, beet roots, turnips, and rutabagas take well to pressure cooking. Normally these roots and tubers can take 1 to 2 hours to cook. In the pressure cooker, cooking times depend on the size of the pieces, not the number of pieces. This means that a large whole vegetable will take longer to cook than the same one cut into 1-inch cubes. And remember, the longer a food cooks, the more water it will need.
- If you like your vegetables soft, or if you are going to purée them, cook for a slightly longer time.
- Always cool cooker quickly under cold running water.
- Delicate vegetables should be cooked using a trivet or placed inside a bowl. Greens should always be cooked just until high pressure is reached.

(continues)

- When pressure steaming on a trivet, make sure the vegetables do not touch the sides of the cooker. They will absorb heat from the walls of the cooker and burn or overcook where they touch.
- Several different vegetables with similar cooking times may be cooked at the same time if the rack or trivet is used. The steam will not carry flavors.
- If you want vegetable flavors to mix, do not use the trivet, which suspends the food above the liquid. Instead set the vegetables right in the cooking liquid so it can carry and mingle flavors.

FRESH VEGETABLE COOKING TIMES

Vegetable	Size	Minutes Cooking at High Pressure*
artichoke, globe	whole	9–11
asparagus	spears or 1" pieces	0–2½
beans, green or wax	whole or cut	1–3
beans, lima	whole	¾–1
beets	small, whole	11–13
	large, whole	15–18
broccoli	florets	2–4
brussels sprouts	whole	5
cabbage, green or red	shredded	2–3
	wedges	5–8
carrots	whole	3–5
	sliced	2
cauliflower	whole	6–8
	florets	2–3
celery	sliced	3–5
collards and kale	2" pieces	4–6
corn	kernels	3
	on the cob	4–5
eggplant	1" cubes	3
greens	whole leaves	1–4
kohlrabi	1" cubes	3–4
onions	whole	6–9
	sliced	3
parsnips	halved	6–8
	½" slices	1–2
peas	whole	0–2
potatoes	whole, medium	12–15
	½" slices	2–3
	halved	8–10
potatoes, sweet or yam	whole, medium	10–11
	halved	8–10
pumpkins	wedge	8–10
rutabagas and turnips	½" slices	3–5
squash, acorn	halved	6–7
squash, hubbard	1" cubes	8–10
squash, summer or zucchini	1" slices	2–3
sweet peppers	whole	1–3
tomatoes	whole	2–3

* A "0 minutes" cooking time means to cook vegetabels just until high pressure is reached. Remove from heat, cool quickly under running water and remove lid immediately.

Fruits

If at all possible, use only organic produce. If organic is not available, scrub all fruit in warm soapy water to remove surface pesticides and trim off any damaged spots, edges, or leaves. Peel any fruit that has been waxed, such as apples.

Fruits of choice (see table)

Place fruits and cooking liquid in pressure cooker (check your cooker's manual for minimum amounts of water). Bring to high pressure quickly. Lower heat and cook for the appropriate time (see table). Be sure to set your timer, as fruits cook fast. Quickly release pressure under cold running water.

These times are approximate. How fast fruit cooks depends upon the degree of ripeness and, in the case of dried fruits, the degree of rehydration. Dried fruit can be rehydrated in water, juices, and liquors, and can be flavored with extracts such as rum, vanilla, and almond. Dried fruit can be presoaked for 30 to 60 minutes.

TIPS FOR FRUIT

- Do not fill cooker more than half full.
- Make sure that poaching fruit does not touch the sides of the pan. The fruit may burn where it touches the cooker.
- Seasonings such as allspice, whole cloves, coriander, cinnamon, ginger, lavender, mint, and nutmeg work well with stewed dried fruit.
- Lime and lemon add high notes to stewed fruit.

COOKING TIMES

Fruit	Minutes Cooking
FRESH	
apples°	4–6
apricots°	5–7
bananas°	6–7
berries°	4–6
cherries°	5–6
cranberries°	4–6
oranges°°	2
peach halves°	3
pears°	6–8
pineapple°°	6–8
plum halves°	4–6
DRIED	
apple rings	6
apricots	3
cranberries	5
dates	10
figs°°°	10
mixed fruit	10
peaches	4–5
pears	8–10
prunes	5–6
raisins	5

° Time given is for cooking in a separate cooking dish.

°° Time given is for poaching on trivet. For cooking in separate dish add 4 to 5 minutes.

°°° Must be presoaked.

- Add a few small pieces of fresh fruit to dishes made with dried fruit.
- If you want to sweeten the fruit, add sugar, honey, or molasses after cooking. Thick sweeteners can stick to the bottom of the pan and burn under pressure. Syrups can also delay the absorption of water into dried fruit and prolong the cooking time.

Basic Dishes

4

THE
ENDLESS
CASSEROLE

Casseroles have always been the mainstay of potlucks and church suppers, but now they are regaining their popularity with busy families. Moms and dads can make several casseroles over the week-end to freeze for use later in the week. Casseroles are easy to cook and serve. Just toss together a green salad and you have a delicious, nutritious, economical meal. Casseroles are good places to hide leftovers and fresh vegetables past their peak. In or out of the house, these recipes will delight the palates of the vegetarian and non-vegetarian alike. Casseroles can be dressed up or dressed down. They can be elegant, festive, or casual, depending on the ingredients you use.

GUIDELINES FOR GREAT CASSEROLES

- Limit the number of ingredients you use in each category. For example, do not use three kinds of beans, two types of grains, and a half dozen different vegetables seasoned with two types of sauces. Too many ingredients will cancel out the flavors.

- Design your casseroles with a variety of textures and complementary flavors. Keep eye appeal in mind as well.

- Brown garlic, onions, fresh mushrooms, carrots, leeks, and scallions before adding to casserole. Sauté in the open pressure cooker to reduce the amount of cookware to clean.

- Mellow out strong vegetables with mild-tasting grains.

- For a high note, add freshly squeezed lemon juice, lime juice, freshly grated lemon zest, or vinegar.

- For a sweet note, add raisins, dried cranberries, or dried apple rings.

- For crunchiness, add sliced water chestnuts, peanuts, or poppy seeds.

- Mix 1 or 2 beaten eggs or egg whites into the casserole for extra firmness.

- For a change, try dry-roasting sesame seeds, quinoa, buckwheat, millet, teff, and amaranth before cooking.

- Make your casserole more than a one-nighter. Put leftovers into a clean casserole dish, add more vegetables, dress up with different seasonings, reheat in pressure cooker for 5 minutes, and then put on another layer of topping.

TAKE YOUR CASSEROLE ON A
TRIP AROUND THE WORLD

For a hint of Italy   tomatoes, basil, mozzarella, Parmesan, pesto, arborio rice, garlic, pine nuts, oregano, plum tomatoes, bell peppers, onions, balsamic vinegar.

For a Mediterranean taste   Greek or Spanish olives, extra virgin olive oil, grape leaves, feta cheese, bay leaves, capers, rosemary, eggplant, thyme, rigani (wild Greek oregano), lemons, saffron threads.

For a taste of Thai   coconut milk (preferably lowfat), grated coconut, fish sauce (called *nam pla* in Asian food stores), cilantro, ground coriander seeds, hot basil (also called hairy basil), Thai chiles, turmeric, peppercorns, garlic, cinnamon, cumin, cloves, lemongrass, sweet basil, *kha* (a ginger-like root).

For an Asian flavor   sesame oil, toasted sesame seeds, snow peas, water chestnuts, wasabi (a hot paste or powdered condiment made from the root of the wasabi japonica plant), soba noodles, soy sauce, tamari, miso, mirin (a sweet rice wine), bok choy, shiitake mushrooms, ginger, cashews, hoisin sauce, water chestnuts.

For a hint of Mexico   chiles (including jalapeños and pastilles), corn, cumin, tomatillos, tomatoes, chili powder, taco shells.

The Endless Casserole

This chapter features our favorite recipe. We like to think of it as "The Endless Casserole," since we never manage to make exactly the same casserole twice. Measuring is not terribly important here; just throw in what looks good to you at the moment. We have been known to make a casserole just as a vehicle for garlic.

1	cup cooked legumes	1	cup sauce (pages 42–43)
2	cups cooked grain or root	1/4	to 1/2 cup seasoning
1 1/2	cups raw vegetable		Topping to taste (page 44)

First choose the protein base for your creation. For a complete protein, a standard ratio is 1 cup cooked legumes to 2 cups cooked grains. (Instructions for cooking legumes and grains can be found in chapter 3.) Well-rinsed canned beans can be substituted for fresh beans if time is a problem. Foods made from soybeans, such as tofu and tempeh, can be substituted for legumes. Instead of grains, occasionally substitute tuber vegetables such as potatoes and yams.

Select one or two vegetables, keeping texture, color, and flavor in mind.

The sauce melds the varying textures and flavors together. As the casserole cooks the sauce sets, firming up the loose ingredients.

It is the job of the seasonings to breathe life into your creation. Hot peppers, garlic, chili powder, and curry powder all define the food they are cooked with.

Layer ingredients in a glass casserole dish that fits easily into the pressure cooker. Be careful not to fill the dish more than two-thirds full to allow room for expansion. Cover the dish with a lid or wax paper and secure. We have found that an ovenproof glass casserole dish with a glass cover works best.

Legumes	Grain or Root
bean sprouts, uncooked	amaranth
black-eyed peas	barley
broad beans	brown rice
cannellini beans	buckwheat (kasha)
garbanzo beans (chickpeas)	bulgur wheat
kidney beans	dry bread cubes
lentils	millet
lima beans	oat groats
pinto beans	quinoa
soybeans	rolled grains
split peas	sweet potatoes, cubed
tempeh	wheat/rye berries
tofu	white potatoes, cubed
white (navy) beans	yams, cubed

Raw Vegetables	Sauce	Seasonings
broccoli	cheese sauce	bell peppers, sautéed
carrots	confetti sauce	celery, sautéed
cauliflower	cottage/ricotta cheese	brewer's yeast
corn	curry sauce	dried mushrooms
eggplant	horseradish sauce	ginger
greens, chopped	lemon sauce	green onions, sautéed
parsnips	miso sauce	herbs, dried/fresh
peas	mustard sauce	horseradish
red cabbage	onion sauce	hot peppers
rutabagas	pesto sauce	leeks, sautéed
squash	red pepper sauce	lemon/lime juice
tomatoes	tofu sauce	miso
turnips	tomato sauce	mustard, dried
zucchini	white sauce	onions and garlic, sautéed
	yogurt sauce	sea vegetables
		sesame salt
		sherry/wine
		sun-dried tomatoes
		tahini
		tamari/soy sauce
		vegetable bouillon
		vegetable juice
		vinegar

Pour 1 to 2 cups water into the cooker. Place trivet inside, set covered casserole on top of trivet, and seal cooker. Bring to high pressure on medium heat and cook for 15 minutes. Reduce pressure slowly for 5 minutes, then cool quickly under cold running water.

For a crunchy crust, add topping ingredients after cooking and place under broiler for a few minutes until top is slightly browned.

The Endless Casserole

Sauces

These recipes can be flavored with almost any seasonings to produce distinct sauces. We include a grain-based sauce, a yogurt-based sauce, and a vegetable-based sauce. When time is a problem, check the bottled sauces available in your health food store or the gourmet food section of your local supermarket.

The milks, yogurts, and cheeses used in these recipes can be made from cow or goat milk or soymilk.

BASIC WHITE SAUCE
(DAIRY-FREE)
MAKES ABOUT 1 CUP

1   tablespoon canola oil, safflower oil, or butter
3   tablespoons whole wheat pastry flour (or 1 teaspoon arrowroot powder)
1   cup plain unsweetened soymilk

2   teaspoons mirin or sherry
3   cloves garlic, minced (about 1½ teaspoons)
    Salt and freshly ground black pepper to taste

In saucepan over low flame, heat oil and mix in flour. Using whisk, stir constantly while gradually adding soymilk, mirin, and garlic. Stir until sauce is smooth and thick. Season with salt and pepper.

Variation *For Cheese Sauce add to the basic recipe after cooking:*

½   cup grated cheese, such as Parmesan, blue, cheddar or Swiss

Pinch ground mustard

Basic Yogurt Sauce

Makes about 1 cup

Remember, the yogurt used in this recipe can be made from cow or goat milk or soymilk.

1	cup plain lowfat yogurt	1	teaspoon honey
1	to 2 cloves garlic, crushed	1/4	teaspoon salt

Combine yogurt, garlic, honey, and salt. Stir until thoroughly blended.

Variations

For Herb Yogurt Sauce add:

1	tablespoon chopped fresh basil	1	tablespoon chopped fresh tarragon

For Horseradish Sauce add:

1   tablespoon prepared horseradish

Vegetable Sauce

Makes about 1 cup

1	cup steamed vegetables (carrots, broccoli, sweet potatoes, white potatoes, or a combination)	1/2	to 1 teaspoon vegetable seasoning Salt and freshly ground black pepper to taste

Combine vegetables, seasoning, salt, and pepper in blender or food processor and process until smooth.

Variation *For Creamy Vegetable Sauce, blend in yogurt, cottage cheese, ricotta cheese, soy cheese, or tofu to taste.*

TOPPINGS

The best part of a casserole is the crunchy top. This recipe will provide that crowning touch.

Take ½ cup from this group

    bread crumbs of any type bread

    crumbled crackers or pretzels

    croutons of any type bread

    flaked cereal such as corn flakes or spelt flakes, whole or crushed

    rolled grains such as rolled oats, rolled wheat, rolled rye

Mix with ½ cup of this group

    crushed or sliced nuts such as almonds, cashews, filberts (hazel nuts), pine nuts, and peanuts

    seeds such as sesame, sunflower, or pumpkin

    toasted teff, quinoa

For a richer topping, add ¼ cup of this group

    butter

    oil such as canola, safflower, or olive

    grated hard cheese such as Parmesan or Romano

    peanut butter

    tahini (sesame seed butter)

Optional ingredients

    nutritional yeast

    shredded cheese such as cheddar or part-skim mozzarella (remember, a little goes a long way)

    shredded coconut

    raisins, dried cranberries, or chopped dried cherries

    wheat germ

Combine ingredients and spread over top of cooked casserole. Place casserole under broiler for a few minutes until topping is browned or cheese begins to bubble. For a nice touch, sauté dry ingredients with butter and oil or dry-roast seeds and nuts.

5

CHILI
AND
ONE-DISH MEALS

The pressure cooker really excels at making chili and other one-dish meals. It combines the flavors of ingredients and mingles spices, producing dishes that taste like they have been slowly simmering for hours under your tender care and watchful eye. All of the recipes in this chapter can be reduced proportionately if your cooker can't handle the volume. Just make sure that you have sufficient water to generate steam. Always make extra. These recipes taste even better the second day.

For an interesting presentation, scoop out the soft center of small round bread loaves and serve the chili in the bread shells. Leftovers can be served over pasta, rice, potatoes, or grains.

For those painful tears that come from chopping onions, there is a solution. Chop your onions near an open flame; the gaseous sulfur compounds the onions release will burn off before they can irritate your eyes. A gas burner works best, but if your stove is electric, try lighting a votive candle near your chopping board instead. You will be amazed at how well this technique works.

For general timetables and more cooking information, turn to chapter 3.

NUTRITION TIPS FOR CHILI

- Remember to use lots of garlic, onions, and leeks. These members of the *Allium* family have natural antibiotic properties that will not only make you feel better but can also help your immune system throw off colds.
- Chilies are great places to "hide" vegetables. If your child will not eat carrots, for instance, cut them into very small pieces and they will disappear into the rest of the chili.
- Add vegetable juices to chilies and sauces to increase the nutritional value.
- To increase the protein value of any chili or sauce, add cubes of tofu or crumbled tempeh.
- Chili peppers do not cause ulcers. The active ingredient, capsaicin, may actually help to prevent them, and may also help to increase metabolism and burn off calories.
- Be creative and use any hearty dried bean in place of kidney beans in chili. All beans are lowfat, high-fiber, protein sources.

West Indian Potato-Bean Stew

SERVES 6

A wonderful combination of beans and root vegetables. Serve with sliced red bell pepper and circles of green onions.

2   tablespoons extra virgin olive oil
1   yellow onion, chopped
1   red onion, chopped
5   cloves garlic, sliced
4   cups Vegetable Broth (page 108)
2   cups cooked white beans, such as cannellini (pages 28–29)
2   red potatoes, chopped
2   carrots, chopped
1   yam, chopped
1   teaspoon turmeric
1   cinnamon stick, about 2 inches long
1   package (10 ounces) frozen corn, thawed
1   package (10 ounces) frozen peas, thawed
6   cups cooked long grain brown rice (pages 26–27)

Heat the olive oil in open pressure cooker over medium heat. Sauté both onions and garlic until soft. Add broth, white beans, potatoes, carrots, yam, turmeric, and cinnamon stick. Seal cooker and bring to high pressure on medium heat. Lower heat and cook for 8 minutes. Reduce pressure quickly under cold running water.

Add corn and peas to open pan, stir, and cook for 5 minutes over medium heat. Remove cinnamon stick. Serve over the rice.

Butternut, Beans, and Polenta

We think the garlic in this recipe works best if the heads are first roasted whole in the oven. The roasted garlic is easily squeezed out of the cloves and into the soup. For a more pronounced flavor, or if you're in a hurry, use minced garlic from a jar or chop fresh cloves.

4	whole garlic heads	2	butternut squash (1 pound),
	Extra virgin olive oil		peeled and cut into 2-inch
4	yellow onions, sliced		cubes
1	leek, carefully cleaned and	1	teaspoon salt or soy sauce
	sliced	2	bay leaves
1/2	cup sherry	1	teaspoon dried marjoram
1	tablespoon balsamic vinegar	1	teaspoon dried thyme
4	cups Vegetable Broth	1/2	teaspoon dried savory
	(page 108)	1	teaspoon ground allspice
1	cup dried cannellini or navy	1/2	teaspoon ground nutmeg
	beans, presoaked (page 28)		Chopped fresh tomatoes for
1	cup dried lima beans,		garnish
	presoaked (page 28)	2	cups cooked polenta
			(pages 26–27)

Preheat oven to 375 degrees. Roast garlic heads for 30 minutes. Remove from oven and let cool. Cut 1/4 inch off the top of each bulb, drizzle with olive oil, and squeeze the pulp from the cloves into a small bowl.

In open pressure cooker combine onions, leek, and sherry, and simmer over medium heat for 5 minutes. Add vinegar and continue to cook uncovered until onions turn golden brown. Add broth, cannellini beans, lima beans, squash, garlic pulp, salt, bay leaves, marjoram, thyme, savory, allspice, and nutmeg.

Seal cooker and bring to high pressure slowly. Lower heat and cook for 15 minutes. Reduce pressure slowly. Remove bay leaves and garnish with tomatoes. Serve over the polenta.

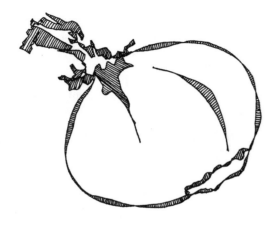

Tempeh and Peppers

SERVES 4

Serve this with warm unseasoned quinoa. This is also a beautiful topping for pasta or potatoes.

3 tablespoons extra virgin olive oil

1 pound plain tempeh, crumbled

1 cup chopped yellow onion

3 cloves garlic, minced

1 red bell pepper, seeded and cut into strips

1 green bell pepper, seeded and cut into strips

1 can (16 ounces) crushed tomatoes with juice

2 tablespoons tomato paste

½ cup red wine

1 teaspoon dried fennel leaves

½ teaspoon dried thyme

1½ teaspoons dried oregano

1 teaspoon dried crushed red pepper

¼ teaspoon paprika

¼ cup minced fresh parsley for garnish

2 cups cooked quinoa (pages 26–27) or 4 baked potatoes

Heat the olive oil in open pressure cooker. Sauté tempeh, onion, garlic, and red and green peppers until pepper strips are soft. Add crushed tomatoes, tomato paste, wine, fennel, thyme, oregano, crushed red pepper, paprika, and ½ cup water.

Seal cooker and bring to high pressure quickly. Lower heat and cook for 10 minutes. Reduce pressure quickly under cold running water.

Simmer with cover off to reduce sauce if necessary. Garnish with parsley. Serve over the quinoa or the baked potatoes.

Chunky Vegetable Chili

SERVES 8

For an interesting variation, leave out the tomato paste and add a dollop of pesto instead.

2	tablespoons extra virgin olive oil		1	cup kidney beans, presoaked (page 28)
5	large mushrooms, sliced		1	can (28 ounces) plum tomatoes with juice, halved
1	zucchini, chopped		1	teaspoon soy sauce or tamari
1	carrot, chopped		2	tablespoons chili powder
1	yellow onion, sliced		1	tablespoon ground allspice
1	cup chopped yellow bell pepper		2	teaspoons ground cumin
3	tablespoons chopped garlic		2	teaspoons dried oregano
3	cups Vegetable Broth (page 108)		1/2	teaspoon freshly ground black pepper
			1	can (8 ounces) tomato paste

Heat the olive oil in open pressure cooker over medium heat. Sauté mushrooms, zucchini, carrot, onion, yellow pepper, and garlic for 5 minutes. Add broth, kidney beans, tomatoes, soy sauce, chili powder, allspice, cumin, oregano, and ground pepper.

Seal cooker and bring to high pressure slowly. Lower heat and cook for 15 minutes. Reduce pressure quickly under cold running water. Add tomato paste, stir, and serve.

White Bean Chili

This recipe can be made more traditional by mashing the beans slightly to thicken the chili, topping with cheddar cheese instead of Parmesan, and serving with crackers.

2	cups cannellini beans, presoaked (page 28)	2	bay leaves
1/4	cup extra virgin olive oil	1/2	cup uncooked bulgur
1	green bell pepper, chopped	2	tablespoons soy sauce or tamari
1	red onion, chopped	10	black Greek olives, pitted
1	yellow onion, chopped	1	cinnamon stick, about 3 inches long
2	tablespoons chopped garlic		
1	green fresh hot chile, sliced		
1	teaspoon chili powder		
1	teaspoon ground cumin		
1	teaspoon dried oregano		
1	teaspoon dried crushed red pepper		

Garnish

Chopped fresh tomatoes
Chopped fresh Italian parsley
Grated Parmesan cheese

In open pressure cooker, cover presoaked beans with water and gently boil for 20 minutes. Drain beans and set aside, discarding liquid.

Heat the olive oil in open cooker over medium heat. Sauté green pepper, both onions, garlic, chile, chili powder, cumin, oregano, crushed red pepper, and bay leaves. Add cooked beans, bulgur, soy sauce, olives, cinnamon stick, and 2 cups water. Seal cooker and bring to high pressure. Lower heat and cook for 10 minutes. Release pressure slowly. Remove bay leaves and cinnamon stick. Garnish with the chopped tomatoes, chopped parsley, and grated Parmesan and serve.

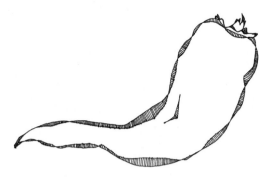

Mild
Three-Bean Chili

SERVES 6

A good recipe for the family with sensitive taste buds. To increase the bite, increase the chili powder, cumin, and crushed red pepper.

2	tablespoons extra virgin olive oil	1	cup dried kidney beans, presoaked (page 28)
1½	cups chopped yellow onions	1	can (8 ounces) tomato paste
3	cloves garlic, minced	½	teaspoon dried oregano
1	can (28 ounces) whole peeled tomatoes with juice, chopped	1	teaspoon chili powder
			Pinch ground cumin
1	cup dried garbanzo beans, presoaked (page 28)		Pinch dried crushed red pepper
1	cup dried black beans, presoaked (page 28)	3	cups Vegetable Broth (page 108) or water

Heat the olive oil in open pressure cooker over medium heat. Sauté onions and garlic until onions are soft. Add tomatoes, garbanzos, black beans, kidney beans, tomato paste, oregano, chili powder, cumin, crushed red pepper, and broth.

Seal cooker and bring to high pressure slowly. Lower heat and cook for 15 minutes. Reduce pressure quickly under cold running water, stir, and serve.

Lentils in Garlic-Tomato Sauce

SERVES 4

Serve over whole grain pasta, noodles, or steamed vegetables.

2 cups Vegetable Broth (page 108)

1 can (28 ounces) whole peeled tomatoes, drained and chopped

1 cup dried lentils, picked over and rinsed

6 cloves garlic, minced
Juice of 1/2 lemon

4 ounces whole wheat spaghetti, cooked

Add broth, tomatoes, lentils, and garlic to pressure cooker. Seal cooker and bring to high pressure. Lower heat and cook for 10 minutes. Reduce pressure quickly under cold running water, stir in lemon juice, and serve over pasta or vegetables.

Chili and One-Dish Meals

Savory Lentil-Potato Stew

SERVES 8

This hearty stew is perfect served alone or with a simple salad.

1/4	cup extra virgin olive oil	1	teaspoon dried oregano
1	large yellow onion, minced	1	teaspoon dried basil
6	red potatoes, diced	5	cups Vegetable Broth
3	carrots, sliced		(page 108)
2	ribs celery, sliced	1/4	cup tamari or soy sauce
1	cup dried lentils, picked over and rinsed	1/2	cup chopped fresh Italian parsley for garnish
1	teaspoon dried savory		

Heat the olive oil in open pressure cooker over medium heat. Sauté onion until soft. Add potatoes, carrots, celery, lentils, savory, oregano, basil, broth, and tamari.

Seal cooker and bring to high pressure over medium heat. Lower heat and cook for 10 minutes. Reduce pressure under cold running water. Stir and garnish with chopped parsley.

Beans with Millet

For a Mediterranean flavor, dress up this simple recipe with a garnish of fresh chopped tomatoes, olives, and crumbled feta cheese.

1 tablespoon extra virgin olive oil

1 yellow onion, diced

1 green bell pepper, diced

1 leek, carefully cleaned and sliced into rounds

3 cups Vegetable Broth (page 108)

1 can (28 ounces) crushed tomatoes

1 cup cannellini beans, presoaked (page 28)

1 cup black beans, presoaked (page 28)

1 cup kidney beans, presoaked (page 28)

6 cups cooked millet (pages 26–27)

Heat the olive oil in open pressure cooker over medium heat. Sauté onion, green pepper, and leek until onion is soft. Add broth, tomatoes, cannellini beans, black beans, and kidney beans.

Seal cooker and bring to high pressure slowly. Lower heat and cook for 25 minutes. Let sit for 5 minutes, then reduce pressure quickly under cold running water. Serve over the millet.

Sautéed Tofu, Vegetables, and Basil

SERVES 6

The tangy vinegar sauce is the key to this tasty vegetable medley.

2	tablespoons extra virgin olive oil		1	cup Vegetable Broth (page 108)
1	pound tofu, cut into 1-inch cubes		5	plum tomatoes, chopped
2	yellow onions, minced			**Sauce**
1	cup bok choy, shredded		⅓	cup balsamic vinegar
2	cups sliced mushrooms		¼	cup extra virgin olive oil
2	teaspoons dried basil		1	tablespoon tamari

Heat the olive oil in open pressure cooker over medium heat. Sauté tofu and onions until tofu begins to brown. Add bok choy, mushrooms, basil, and broth.

Seal cooker and bring to high pressure slowly over medium heat. Lower heat and cook for 2 minutes. Reduce pressure quickly under cold running water. Strain vegetables, discarding liquid, and add tomatoes.

To make sauce, whisk together vinegar, olive oil, and tamari. Toss with tofu-vegetable mixture and serve.

Asian Vegetable Stir-Fry

SERVES 6

1   cup shredded bok choy
1   leek, carefully cleaned and
        sliced into 1/4-inch rounds
1   cup snow peas
1   cup whole shiitake or oyster
        mushrooms
1/2   cup sliced carrots
1/2   cup sliced celery
1/4   cup bamboo shoots
2   cups Vegetable Broth
        (page 108)

1   cup mung bean sprouts
1   can (8 ounces) water
        chestnuts, drained and sliced
2   cups cooked brown rice
        (pages 26–27)

Sauce
2   tablespoons tamari
2   tablespoons sesame seeds
2   tablespoons sesame oil
2   tablespoons rice vinegar

Add bok choy, leek, snow peas, mushrooms, carrots, celery, bamboo shoots, and broth to pressure cooker.

Seal cooker and bring to high pressure quickly. Lower heat and cook for 3 minutes. Reduce pressure quickly under cold running water. Strain vegetables, discarding liquid, and add sprouts and water chestnuts.

To make sauce, whisk together tamari, seeds, oil, and vinegar. Toss with cooked vegetables and serve over the brown rice.

Sweet and Sour Stir-Fry Vegetables

SERVES 4

1 red bell pepper, seeded and cut into strips	**Sauce**
1 green bell pepper, seeded and cut into strips	2 cloves garlic, crushed
3 ribs celery, sliced	1/4 cup grated fresh ginger
1 can (8 ounces) water chestnuts, drained	1/4 cup tamari or soy sauce
1 cup blanched, sliced almonds	1/4 cup freshly squeezed lemon juice
2 cups sliced button mushrooms	1 tablespoon balsamic vinegar
2 cups cooked brown rice (pages 26–27)	2 tablespoons honey

Add both peppers, celery, water chestnuts, almonds, mushrooms, and 2 cups water to pressure cooker. Seal cooker and bring to high pressure quickly. Lower heat and cook for 2 minutes. Reduce pressure quickly under cold running water. Strain vegetables, discarding liquid.

To make sauce, whisk together garlic, ginger, tamari, lemon juice, vinegar, and honey. Toss with cooked vegetables and serve over the brown rice.

6

VEGETABLE
SIDE
DISHES

Pressure cooking brings out the flavors and textures of vegetables while preventing the escape of cooking odors. It is the best method for cooking root vegetables such as potatoes, rutabagas, turnips, carrots, parsnips, and yams, transforming them from rock hard to moist and tender.

For perfectly cooked vegetables, bring them to high pressure quickly. Precision timing is essential. Since you cannot take the lid off to check the progress, it is easiest to use the cooking chart and time the cooking exactly. As little as half a minute at such high temperatures can make all the difference. When timing, aim for underdone rather than overdone. Vegetable timetables can be found in chapter 3.

Vegetable Sauces

Dress up your pressure-cooked vegetables with one of these easy hot sauces. Use any kind of milk, yogurt, or cheese you like, and choose regular, lowfat, or nonfat. For a crowning touch, dust the top of a dish with crushed nuts, seeds, grated cheese, or croutons. For additional sauce ideas, turn to chapter 4.

CREAMY DILL SAUCE
MAKES ABOUT 1 CUP

1 cup lowfat milk of choice
2 tablespoons chopped green onions (about 1 to 2 green onions)
¼ teaspoon dried dill

1 tablespoon arrowroot powder mixed with 2 tablespoons cold milk
Salt and freshly ground black pepper to taste

In open pressure cooker or saucepan, combine milk, green onions, dill, arrowroot mixture, salt, and black pepper. Mix well. Cook over medium heat, stirring constantly, until sauce starts to thicken. Serve warm over cooked vegetables.

HOT CURRY SAUCE

MAKES 1 CUP

1 cup nonfat yogurt (or
   3/4 cup nonfat yogurt plus
   1/4 cup lowfat mayonnaise)

1/2 teaspoon curry powder
1/2 teaspoon prepared mustard

Combine yogurt, curry powder, and mustard in small saucepan. Stirring constantly, heat almost to boiling and serve hot over vegetables.

CHEESE SAUCE

MAKES ABOUT 1 CUP

1/2 cup milk of choice
1/2 cup plain lowfat yogurt
1 tablespoon cornstarch mixed
   with a few tablespoons of
   the milk

Pinch dry mustard
Salt and freshly ground
   black pepper to taste
1/4 cup grated or shredded
   cheese of choice

In a saucepan combine milk, yogurt, cornstarch slurry, dry mustard, salt, and black pepper. Heat until thickened, stirring constantly; do not let boil. Remove from heat and stir in cheese. Serve immediately over vegetables.

(continues)

HOT TOFU SAUCE
MAKES ABOUT 1 CUP

½ pound soft tofu
Choose one of the following flavor combinations:
2 tablespoons chopped yellow onion and 1 tablespoon powdered vegetable stock

2 tablespoons freshly squeezed lemon juice and 2 teaspoons prepared mustard
½ cup thawed frozen spinach and 1 teaspoon honey and 1 chopped green onion

Place tofu and desired flavor combination in a blender and process until smooth. Pour into a small saucepan and heat until almost boiling, stirring frequently. Serve immediately over vegetables.

HOT YOGURT SAUCE
MAKES ABOUT 1 CUP

1 cup plain yogurt
Choose one of the following flavor combinations:
½ teaspoon curry powder and ½ teaspoon prepared mustard
½ teaspoon chili powder and ¼ teaspoon ground cumin and pinch of dried crushed red pepper

2 tablespoons tamari and 1 tablespoon sesame seeds and ¼ teaspoon ground ginger
⅓ cup packed fresh mint leaves, minced and 2 teaspoons honey
½ cup shredded sharp cheddar cheese and pinch of dry mustard

Combine yogurt and desired flavor combination in a small saucepan and heat almost to boiling, stirring frequently. Serve immediately over vegetables.

New Potato Salad

Serve this potato salad warm for a new take on an old favorite.

6   cups cubed (1-inch) new
    potatoes
½   cup diced celery
½   cup diced red onion
½   cup diced green onion

½   cup minced fresh parsley
½   cup Italian dressing
2   tablespoons freshly squeezed
    lemon juice

Special Equipment
Well-oiled trivet

Pour 1 cup water into pressure cooker and place trivet inside. Lay potatoes on trivet. Seal cooker and bring to high pressure quickly. Lower heat and cook for 7 minutes. Reduce pressure quickly under cold running water.

Toss potatoes with celery, red onion, green onion, parsley, Italian dressing, and lemon juice. Serve warm or chilled.

Curried Eggplant

SERVES 6

Try a seasonal squash in place of the eggplant. Add 1 tablespoon mixed curry to the spices if you prefer a stronger curry flavor.

2	tablespoons extra virgin olive oil	1	can (28 ounces) whole peeled tomatoes with juice, chopped
1	eggplant, cut into 2-inch cubes	1	package (10 ounces) frozen peas
1	yellow onion, diced	1	tablespoon freshly squeezed lemon juice
6	cloves garlic, minced	1	teaspoon salt
1	teaspoon turmeric		
1	teaspoon ground cumin		
1/2	teaspoon dried crushed red pepper		

Heat the olive oil in open pressure cooker. Sauté eggplant with onion, garlic, turmeric, cumin, and crushed red pepper, until onions soften. Add tomatoes with their juice. Seal cooker and bring to high pressure quickly. Lower heat and cook for 3 minutes. Reduce pressure quickly under cold running water.

Add peas, lemon juice, and salt. Cook in open cooker until peas are warmed through, about 5 minutes. Serve over pasta or whole grains such as polenta, quinoa, or brown rice.

Artichokes and Dip

To prepare artichokes for cooking, cut about 2 inches off their prickly tops and remove the tough stems.

3   medium globe artichokes

Horseradish Dip
1   piece of fresh horseradish root
    (3 inches long), peeled and
    grated
¼   cup mayonnaise, yogurt, or
    silken tofu

Special Equipment
Well-oiled trivet

Pour 1 cup water into pressure cooker and place trivet inside. Set the artichokes upside down on trivet so the steam rises up into leaves. Seal cooker and bring to high pressure quickly. Lower heat and cook for 10 minutes. Reduce pressure quickly under cold running water.

   To make dip, combine horseradish and mayonnaise in a small bowl and mix well. Serve beside the artichokes.

Variation   *Place the artichokes right side up in the pressure cooker. Sprinkle 1 tablespoon freshly squeezed lemon juice and 1 teaspoon dried oregano onto each artichoke. Cook as above.*

Caramelized Root Vegetables

SERVES 4

Vegetables lightly coated in a sweet glaze are the perfect side dish for any meal.

1	tablespoon honey	1	peeled yam, coarsely chopped
1½	cups Vegetable Broth (page 108)	2	tablespoons butter
1	carrot, coarsely chopped	¼	cup chopped Italian parsley
1	parsnip, coarsely chopped		

Dissolve honey in ½ cup of the broth. Add honey mixture to pressure cooker along with the remaining broth, carrot, parsnip, yam, and butter. Seal cooker and bring to high pressure quickly. Lower heat and cook for 3 minutes. Reduce pressure quickly under cold running water.

Return open cooker to heat and reduce sauce until butter and honey begin to caramelize. Gently toss vegetables to coat with glaze, stir in parsley, and serve.

Herbed Parsnips

Introduce this underappreciated vegetable to your family with this delicate dish.

10	medium parsnips, peeled and quartered	$1/4$	cup minced fresh Italian parsley
3	tablespoons butter	$1/2$	teaspoon dried basil

Add parsnips and 2 cups water to pressure cooker. Seal cooker and bring to high pressure quickly. Lower heat and cook for 5 minutes. Reduce pressure quickly under cold running water.

Drain the parsnips. Slice into thin strips and toss with butter, parsley, and basil. Serve warm.

Jalapeños, Onions, and Green Beans

SERVES 6

For a brighter flavor, substitute freshly squeezed lemon juice for the vinegar. A sliced yellow onion can be used in place of the pearl onions.

2	cups string beans, washed and topped	1	jalapeño pepper, seeded and minced
10	pearl onions	1	red chile pepper, seeded and minced
5	cloves garlic, sliced	3	tablespoons balsamic vinegar
1	can (28 ounces) whole peeled tomatoes, drained and chopped		

Special Equipment
Well-oiled trivet

Pour 1 cup water into pressure cooker and place trivet inside. Combine beans, onions, garlic, tomatoes, jalapeño, and chile and lay on trivet. Seal cooker and bring to high pressure quickly. Lower heat and cook for 5 minutes. Reduce pressure quickly under cold running water. Splash balsamic vinegar over the vegetables and serve.

Sweet
Acorn Squash

SERVES 4

A hit with the kids. Seasonal squash can be used as a substitute in this nutritionally rich treat.

1	tablespoon extra virgin olive oil	1/4	cup chopped dehydrated apple slices
1	medium acorn squash, seeds removed, cut lengthwise and sliced into 3/4-inch-thick half moons	1/3	cup apple juice
		1	tablespoon molasses
		1/4	teaspoon ground nutmeg
			Dash of salt

Lightly coat bottom of the pressure cooker with olive oil and layer with squash slices. Add apples, apple juice, molasses, nutmeg, and salt. Seal cooker and bring to high pressure over medium heat. Lower heat and cook for 8 to 10 minutes. Reduce pressure quickly under cold running water. Stir and serve.

Garlic Mashed Potatoes

SERVES 6

This German favorite is irresistable. Sealed leftovers will keep for up to a week in the refrigerator.

6	russet potatoes, halved	¼	cup (½ stick) butter
2	cups whole milk	¼	cup minced garlic

Add potatoes and 4 cups water to pressure cooker. Seal cooker and bring to high pressure quickly. Lower heat and cook for 8 minutes. Reduce pressure quickly under cold running water, or let fall on its own.

Strain off excess water and add milk, butter, and garlic to potatoes in open cooker. Mash well, adding more milk if necessary, and serve.

Confetti Potatoes

This recipe also works well with yams. If you are using organic produce leave the skins on. All others should be peeled.

3	medium white potatoes, cut into 1/4-inch slices	1	tablespoon chopped red bell pepper
1	large sweet potato, cut into 1/4-inch slices	1	tablespoon chopped yellow bell pepper
1	cup nonfat yogurt (soy, goat, or dairy)	1	tablespoon chopped green onion
1/4	cup salsa		

Special Equipment

Well-oiled trivet

Pour 1 cup water into pressure cooker and place trivet inside. Lay all potato slices on top of trivet. Seal cooker and bring to high pressure quickly. Lower heat and cook for 4 minutes. Let cooker sit for 5 minutes off heat, then reduce pressure quickly under cold running water.

Arrange potato slices on a warm platter. Mix yogurt and salsa and pour over potatoes. Sprinkle peppers and green onion over the top. Serve warm.

Spicy Cauliflower

SERVES 4

This traditional East Indian dish can be made in minutes and will impress your friends and family.

2	heads cauliflower, cut into florets	1	teaspoon coriander seeds
¼	cup extra virgin olive oil	2	cardamom pods
1	large yellow onion, chopped	1	teaspoon turmeric

Add cauliflower and 1 cup water to pressure cooker. Seal cooker and bring to high pressure quickly. Lower heat and cook for 3 minutes. Reduce pressure quickly under cold running water. Drain and set cauliflower aside.

Heat the olive oil in open pressure cooker over medium heat. Sauté onion until browning begins. Add coriander and cardamom and sauté for 5 minutes. This releases the flavor from the spices into the oil. Add turmeric and cauliflower, toss, and serve.

Asian Vegetables

Stir-fry strips of miso-flavored tempeh to turn this dish into a main entrée. Serve over a plate of noodles or in a noodle soup.

1	cup broccoli florets	1½	teaspoons cornstarch dissolved in 1 tablespoon water
1	cup sliced carrots		
½	cup sliced water chestnuts	1	teaspoon grated fresh ginger
½	cup sliced red bell pepper	1	small clove garlic, minced
1	tablespoon soy sauce		

Special Equipment

Well-oiled trivet

Pour 1 cup water into pressure cooker and place trivet inside. Lay broccoli, carrots, water chestnuts, and red pepper on trivet. Seal cooker and bring to high pressure quickly. Lower heat and cook for 5 minutes. Reduce pressure quickly under cold running water. Remove vegetables to warm bowl and discard all but ½ cup of cooking liquid.

Add soy sauce, cornstarch slurry, ginger, and garlic to open cooker and cook, stirring frequently, until thickened. Return vegetables to cooker and toss until coated with sauce.

Asian Carrots

This bright, tasty vegetable dish goes well with almost any grain or bean dish.

4	carrots, peeled and halved lengthwise	2	tablespoons sesame oil
4	green onions, trimmed and sliced	2	tablespoons tamari or soy sauce
1	bunch watercress, chopped	2	tablespoons sesame seeds

Add carrots and 2 cups water to pressure cooker. Seal cooker and bring to high pressure quickly. Lower heat and cook for 2 minutes. Reduce pressure quickly under cold running water.

Drain liquid from cooker and add green onions, watercress, and sesame oil. Sauté for 3 minutes in open cooker. Add tamari and sesame seeds, toss, and serve.

Company Carrots

SERVES 4

Nice enough for guests but simple enough to serve every day. Any slightly fruity wine, such as Sauvignon Blanc or Johannesburg Riesling, can be substituted for the Zinfandel.

1	pound whole, small, narrow carrots (about 5 inches long)	½	cup Vegetable Broth (page 108)
1	cup White Zinfandel	1	teaspoon butter

Add carrots, wine, broth, and butter to pressure cooker. Seal cooker and bring to high pressure quickly. Lower heat and cook for 3 minutes. Reduce pressure quickly under cold running water. Return open cooker to heat and simmer to reduce cooking liquid until carrots brown. Serve.

Beans and Salsa

A quick and easy dish that goes well with a savory bean or rice entrée.

3	medium carrots, cut into 4-inch sticks	1	cup whole wax beans
1	cup whole green beans	½	cup red salsa

Special Equipment
Well-oiled trivet

Pour 1 cup water into pressure cooker and place trivet inside. Lay carrots, green beans, and wax beans on trivet. Seal cooker and bring to high pressure quickly. Lower heat and cook for 5 minutes. Reduce pressure quickly under cold running water.

Strain vegetables, place in a warm bowl, and top with salsa.

Quick Vegetable Plate

SERVES 4

Vegetables can be done in about 2 minutes. If you like your vegetables well cooked, add another minute. The vegetables can be cooked in a glass casserole dish that goes from cooker to table.

12	baby carrots, cut in half lengthwise	8	thin asparagus stalks
12	small florets cauliflower	16	wax beans, sliced in half lengthwise
12	small florets broccoli		

Special Equipment
Well-oiled trivet
Glass casserole dish with cover (optional)

Pour 1 cup water into pressure cooker and place trivet inside. Arrange vegetables on trivet. If using a casserole dish, be sure to cover it.

Seal cooker and bring to high pressure quickly. Lower heat and cook for 2 to 3 minutes. Reduce pressure quickly under cold running water. Strain liquid from vegetables and serve immediately.

Vegetable Curry

SERVES 4

A taste of India from Ireland. Maureen picked up this recipe from her Irish sister-in-law, Lena.

2 teaspoons mustard seeds, any color	2 tablespoons tomato paste
2 teaspoons coriander seeds	¾ cup Vegetable Broth (page 108)
2 teaspoons cumin seeds	2 medium potatoes, cut into 1-inch cubes
2 tablespoons extra virgin olive oil	1 medium-large sweet potato, cut into 1-inch cubes
1 large yellow onion, thinly sliced	4 medium carrots, cut into 1-inch slices
3 cloves garlic, minced	
2 teaspoons minced fresh ginger	2 medium zucchini, cut into 1-inch cubes
1½ teaspoons turmeric	
½ teaspoon chili powder	1 cup chopped fresh spinach
1 can (16 ounces) whole peeled tomatoes with juice, chopped	2 tablespoons lowfat coconut milk

In open dry pressure cooker, gently toast mustard seeds, coriander seeds, and cumin seeds for 2 minutes. Crush with the back of a wooden spoon. Remove from cooker and set aside.

Add olive oil to cooker and sauté onions and garlic until softened. Add crushed spices, ginger, turmeric, and chili powder and continue to cook for 2 to 3 minutes. Mix in tomatoes, tomato paste, broth, potatoes, sweet potato, and carrots.

Seal cooker and bring to high pressure quickly. Lower heat and cook for 1½ minutes. Reduce pressure quickly under cold running water.

Add zucchini and spinach. Seal cooker and bring again to high pressure. Lower heat and cook for another 1½ minutes. Reduce pressure quickly under cold running water.

With a slotted spoon, remove vegetables to a warm plate. Boil remaining liquid in open cooker to reduce to a sauce. Adjust seasoning, stir in coconut milk, and simmer for 1 minute. Pour sauce over vegetables.

Braised Red Cabbage and Pearl Onions

SERVES 4

Sautéing in butter gives these vegetables a carmelized sweetness. Lemon juice dressing balances this flavor harmoniously.

2	tablespoons butter	1	red cabbage, sliced into rounds
1	cup pearl onions, peeled	2	tablespoons freshly squeezed lemon juice
1	tablespoon chopped garlic		

Heat the butter in open pressure cooker over medium heat. Sauté onions and garlic until onions begins to brown. Add cabbage and 1 cup water.

Seal cooker and bring to high pressure quickly. Lower heat and cook for 2 minutes. Reduce pressure quickly under cold running water. Strain and toss with lemon juice.

Red Cabbage

A spicy dish that goes well with a casserole.

2	tablespoons extra virgin olive oil	2	medium cooking apples, sliced
1	medium yellow onion, sliced	3	whole cloves
1/4	cup red wine	2	tablespoons cider vinegar
1	red cabbage, shredded	1	tablespoon brown sugar
		1/4	teaspoon ground allspice

Heat the olive oil in open pressure cooker over medium heat. Sauté onion until soft. Add wine, cabbage, apples, and cloves in that order so apples rest on top of cabbage.

Seal cooker and bring to high pressure quickly. Lower heat and cook for 2 minutes. Reduce pressure quickly under cold running water.

Remove cloves and add vinegar, brown sugar, and allspice. Stir over heat for 1 minute. Serve.

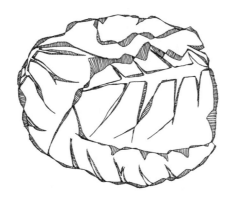

Vegetable Side Dishes

7

GRAIN AND LEGUME SIDE DISHES

Staple foods such as whole grains and beans usually require hours of slow cooking before they are ready to eat. The pressure cooker cuts this time in half or less and makes these vegetarian dishes into fast foods. Forget to soak the beans? No problem. Just toss them in the cooker to pressure soak. In less than 10 minutes they are ready for cooking (see page 28).

If you are one of those cooks who burns the brown rice because it takes so long that you get busy with something else and forget to check it, then pressure cooking is the answer for you. Forget the nutritionally depleted instant rice, and pressure steam flavorful whole grains.

Timetables and instructions for cooking grains and legumes can be found in chapter 3. To avoid possible clogging of the vent pipe with foam and bean skins, do not fill the cooker more than one-third full of soaked beans, grains, and liquid. Adding 1 tablespoon vegetable oil to the cooking water will help lubricate the vent pipe and keep loose bean skins from clogging it.

GRAIN NUTRITION FACTS

- According to the USDA's new Food Pyramid, grains should form the basis of the healthy diet. It is recommended that we eat at least 6 servings of whole grains each day.

- Eat a variety of grains. Do not limit yourself to brown rice. Each grain has its unique nutritional value.

- To ensure that your family gets enough protein, serve grains with beans, soybean products, or dairy foods.

- Whole grains are a nutritional powerhouse. They are excellent sources of both soluble and insoluble fiber and trace minerals such as zinc and selenium. If you suffer from diabetes, high blood cholesterol, or irregularity, always cook with whole grains.

LEGUME NUTRITION FACTS

- Legumes are an excellent source of protein. When served with grains, vegetables, or dairy products, they provide all the amino acids the body needs.

- Legumes are the perfect diet food. Rich in fiber and complex carbohydrates, but low in fat and calories, they fill up the stomach without filling out the waist.

- The soluble fiber in legumes can reduce high cholesterol levels and may aid in the prevention of colon cancer.

- Legumes keep blood-sugar levels even, making them an important food for people with diabetes or hypoglycemia.
- Worried about the aluminum content of your cooker? Place a trivet or rack inside the cooker and add water. Fit a stainless steel bowl or ovenproof glass dish into the cooker. Add pre-soaked beans and an equal amount of water to the dish. Cover the container securely to prevent condensation from diluting the cooking liquid and cook a few minutes longer than directed.
- Canned and dried beans can be used in the pressure cooker. Canned beans require only about 2 minutes to heat through. All beans—fresh, dried, or canned—are nutritionally rich and a healthful addition to any meal.

TAKING THE GAS OUT OF BEANS

Beans contain sugars of the raffinose family that the human digestive tract cannot easily digest. These compounds eventually work their way to the large intestine where they are digested by the bacteria that populate the region. Gas is one of the by-products of this biochemical process. There are many tricks for reducing gas, some more successful than others.

- Eat a steady diet of beans and hope your body will eventually get used to dealing with them. After 4 or 5 days of consistent intake of legumes, your body will begin to expect them and compensate by producing the enzymes needed to thoroughly digest them. This does work for some. The trick is to eat legumes every day.
- Add a piece of kombu—a tasty sea vegetable—to the cooking beans. This is said to increase their digestibility along with adding flavor.
- Discard the soaking water and rinse beans well. The flatulent sugars are water soluble.
- Do not soak your beans overnight. Use the quick-soak method (page 28). Overnight soaking just causes the beans to make more of the gas-causing substances.
- Several new products on the market provide the enzymes necessary for digesting the offensive sugars. Just swallow a tablet or drip a liquid onto the first bite and eat as many beans as you like. They are available in health food stores and pharmacies.

Grain and Legume Side Dishes

Basic
Beans

SERVES 4

This recipe makes a great side dish or it can be served over grains for an easy entrée. Dress it up by adding a cup of chopped tomatoes, a half cup of Greek olives and a half cup chopped sun-dried tomatoes before cooking.

1	tablespoon extra virgin olive oil	1	leek, carefully cleaned and sliced
1	yellow onion, sliced	1	cup cannellini beans, quick-soaked (page 28)
1	red bell pepper, seeded and sliced		

Heat the olive oil in open pressure cooker over medium heat. Sauté onion, red pepper, and leek until soft. Add beans and 1 1/2 cups water.

Seal cooker and bring to high pressure quickly. Lower heat and cook for 7 minutes. Reduce pressure quickly under cold running water.

Puerto Rican Rice and Beans

SERVES 4

Add ½ teaspoon hot chile pepper oil for a spicier version or 1 tablespoon capers or sliced olives for a saltier, Mediterranean twist.

4 cups Vegetable Broth plus ½ cup additional if necessary (page 108)

2 cups white beans, quick-soaked (page 28)

1 can (28 ounces) whole peeled tomatoes with juice, chopped

1 cup uncooked long or medium grain brown rice

2 fresh tomatoes, chopped

1 acorn squash, peeled and cut into 2-inch cubes

1 green bell pepper, chopped

1 Anaheim chile pepper, diced

2 tablespoons extra virgin olive oil

1 tablespoon minced garlic
   Cilantro sprigs for garnish

In pressure cooker, combine 4 cups broth, beans, canned tomatoes, rice, fresh tomatoes, squash, green pepper, chile pepper, olive oil, and garlic.

Seal cooker and bring to high pressure quickly. Lower heat and cook for 30 minutes. Reduce pressure quickly under cold running water. Check beans and rice for doneness.

If more cooking is necessary, add ½ cup more vegetable broth. Reseal cooker and return to high pressure quickly. Lower heat and cook for 5 more minutes. Reduce pressure quickly under cold running water. Repeat this step as necessary.

When cooking is completed, garnish with several sprigs of cilantro and serve.

Moroccan Chickpeas

This recipe can be served cold the next day. We like to mix in leftover rice and stuff the mixture into pita bread.

2	tablespoons extra virgin olive oil	1	cup Vegetable Broth (page 108)
2	medium yellow onions, chopped	1	teaspoon ground cinnamon
1	clove garlic, minced	1	teaspoon turmeric
2	cups chickpeas (garbanzo beans), quick-soaked (page 28)	1/2	teaspoon ground ginger
		1/2	cup raisins
		1/4	cup unsalted whole peanuts

Heat the olive oil in open pressure cooker over medium heat. Sauté onions and garlic until tender. Add chickpeas, broth, cinnamon, turmeric, and ginger.

Seal cooker and bring to high pressure quickly. Lower heat and cook for 11 minutes. Reduce pressure quickly under cold running water.

Mix in raisins and peanuts. Simmer for 5 minutes in open pan before serving.

Black-Eyed Peas and Rice

SERVES 4

A simple recipe, simply seasoned—a perfect comfort food.

1   can (15 ounces) sliced
     tomatoes with juice
1/2 cup uncooked brown rice
1   zucchini, sliced

2   cups black-eyed peas, quick-
     soaked (page 28)
Salt to taste
Black pepper to taste

Add tomatoes, rice, zucchini, and 1/2 cup water to pressure cooker. Seal cooker and bring to high pressure quickly. Lower heat and cook for 20 minutes. Reduce pressure quickly under cold running water.

Add peas. Reseal cooker and return to high pressure. Lower heat and cook for an additional 10 minutes. Reduce pressure quickly under cold running water. Season to taste with salt or freshly ground black pepper.

Sunday Oatmeal

SERVES 2

Our favorite breakfast recipe. Use dried apple slices rather than fresh; fresh, sliced apple turns to applesauce when cooked under pressure. The oatmeal is cooked using pressure steaming, which decreases the chance of scorching and makes cleanup a snap.

1	cup steel-cut oats	½	teaspoon cinnamon
½	cup chopped dehydrated apple slices	¼	cup date sugar

Special Equipment

Trivet

Ovenproof casserole dish with cover

Pour 1 cup water into pressure cooker and place trivet inside. Combine oats, apple, and cinnamon in casserole dish, securely cover, and set on trivet.

Seal cooker and bring to high pressure quickly. Lower heat and cook for 2 minutes. Reduce pressure quickly under cold running water.

Dust each serving with 2 tablespoons date sugar, and serve with soymilk or dairy milk.

Warm Strawberry Quinoa

SERVES 3

A delicious change of pace. Any frozen berry can be substituted for the strawberries. If you want to be really bad, drizzle a bit of high-quality melted chocolate over the quinoa and berries. Yummy!

1	cup uncooked quinoa	1	tablespoon honey
1	cup frozen strawberries		

Special Equipment
Trivet
Ovenproof casserole dish with cover

Pour 1 cup water into the bottom of pressure cooker and place trivet inside. Combine quinoa, frozen strawberries, and 1 cup water in casserole dish, securely cover, and set on trivet.

Seal cooker and bring to high pressure quickly. Lower heat and cook for 5 minutes. Reduce pressure quickly under cold running water.

Spoon the servings into separate bowls and drizzle 1 teaspoon honey on each. Serve.

Italian Polenta

SERVES 6

Polenta is mush made from coarsely ground cornmeal, and is a staple of Northern Italy. Its bright yellow color and fresh corn flavor make it an ideal base for many vegetables dishes.

2	tablespoons extra virgin olive oil	1½	cups coarsely ground cornmeal
10	to 15 pitted whole olives (preferably Greek or green olives)	3	tablespoons capers, rinsed
		2	tablespoons minced fresh thyme
2	tablespoons chopped garlic	1	can (28 ounces) whole peeled tomatoes with juice, chopped
1	teaspoon freshly ground black pepper		
4	cups Vegetable Broth (page 108)	6	tablespoons grated Parmesan cheese

In a sauté pan heat the olive oil over medium heat. Sauté olives, garlic, and black pepper for 5 minutes.

Meanwhile, add broth, cornmeal, capers, and thyme to pressure cooker. Seal cooker and bring to high pressure quickly. Lower heat and cook for 5 minutes. Reduce pressure quickly under cold running water.

Add tomatoes to the sauce in the sauté pan and heat through. Serve sauce over polenta. Sprinkle 1 tablespoon Parmesan cheese over each serving.

Caper Polenta

Capers are the pickled buds of a prickly Mediterranean shrub. Mild polenta complements the strong flavor of cumin and capers. This recipe is featured on the book cover.

2	tablespoons extra virgin olive oil	3½	cups Vegetable Broth (page 108)
1	red onion, sliced	1	cup coarsely ground cornmeal
1	leek, carefully cleaned and sliced	3	tablespoons capers, rinsed
1	large carrot, sliced	1	tablespoon ground cumin
1	red bell pepper, seeded and sliced	1	tablespoon soy sauce

Heat the olive oil in open pressure cooker over medium heat. Sauté onion, leek, carrot, and red pepper for 5 minutes. Add broth, cornmeal, capers, cumin, and soy sauce.

Seal cooker and bring to high pressure quickly. Lower heat and cook for 5 minutes. Allow pressure to fall on its own. Stir and serve with steamed vegetables.

Barley
Provençale

SERVES 4

Barley is a delicious, chewy grain that has been eaten by humans since the Stone Age. The French have used savory vegetables to accent barley's sweet flavor in this traditional country recipe.

1	tablespoon extra virgin olive oil	¾	cup uncooked pearled barley, rinsed
1	large yellow onion, chopped	½	cup chopped Italian parsley
4	cloves garlic, minced	1	tablespoon capers, rinsed
1¼	cups Vegetable Broth (page 108)	1	tablespoon chopped fresh thyme
1	can (28 ounces) crushed tomatoes with liquid	2	cups cooked quinoa (pages 26–27)

Heat the olive oil in open pressure cooker over medium heat. Sauté onion and garlic for 5 minutes. Add broth, tomatoes, barley, parsley, capers, and thyme.

Seal cooker and bring to high pressure quickly. Lower heat and cook for 20 minutes. Release pressure quickly under cold running water. Stir and serve over the quinoa.

Pistachios, Millet, and Onions

SERVES 4

Feel free to improvise with this recipe. The salty nuts and olives balance the mild millet and tomatoes.

2 tablespoons extra virgin olive oil	1 can (28 ounces) stewed tomatoes with liquid, chopped
1 red onion, minced	1/4 cup pistachios
2 cups Vegetable Broth (page 108)	5 Greek olives, sliced
1 1/3 cups uncooked millet	

Heat the olive oil in open pressure cooker over medium heat. Sauté onion for 2 minutes. Add broth, millet, tomatoes, pistachios, and olives.

Seal cooker and bring to high pressure quickly. Lower heat and cook for 10 minutes. Reduce pressure quickly under cold running water.

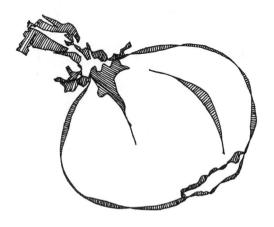

Grain and Legume Side Dishes

Hot Chile, Olive, and Pistachio Rice

SERVES 4

The heat in this recipe comes from the chile peppers. You can vary the fire by modifying the amount of chiles and chili powder you use.

1   cup uncooked aromatic rice
    (basmati or wehani)
1   can (28 ounces) whole peeled
    tomatoes, drained
1½ cups Vegetable Broth
    (page 108)
½   cup whole pitted black olives
1   can (4 ounces) mild green
    chiles

1   green hot chile pepper, sliced
    into rounds
½   cup pistachios
6   cloves garlic, minced
1   tablespoon chili powder

Garnish
½   cup chopped cilantro
3   green onions, sliced
1   lemon, cut into wedges

Add to pressure cooker rice, tomatoes, broth, olives, canned chiles, fresh chile, pistachios, garlic, and chili powder.

Seal cooker and bring to high pressure quickly. Lower heat and cook for 30 minutes. Reduce pressure quickly under cold running water.

Garnish with cilantro, green onion slices, and lemon wedges before serving.

Mushroom Risotto

SERVES 6

Use wild mushrooms such as shiitake or porcini for a stronger flavor.

2   tablespoons extra virgin olive oil

1   red onion, minced

3¾   cups Vegetable Broth (page 108)

1   can (28 ounces) whole peeled tomatoes, drained and chopped

1½   cups uncooked arborio rice

2   cups button mushrooms, cleaned and halved

¼   cup pine nuts

1   teaspoon saffron threads

Heat the olive oil in open pressure cooker over medium heat. Sauté onion for 5 minutes. Add broth, tomatoes, rice, mushrooms, pine nuts, and saffron.

Seal cooker and bring to high pressure quickly. Lower heat and cook for 5 minutes. Remove from heat and let stand for another 5 minutes before reducing pressure under cold running water.

Golden Rice Pilaf

SERVES 4

Delete the oil and nuts for a lower-fat version of this already lowfat recipe. A 1-inch piece of peeled fresh ginger added to the cooking broth brings out a delicate Asian edge.

2	tablespoons extra virgin olive oil	2½	cups Vegetable Broth (page 108)
1	medium yellow onion, chopped	1	cinnamon stick, about 3 inches long
¼	cup pine nuts		Salt and freshly ground black pepper to taste
¼	cup slivered almonds	¼	cup golden raisins
1½	cups uncooked long grain brown rice		

Heat the olive oil in open pressure cooker over medium heat. Sauté onion, pine nuts, and almonds for 3 minutes. Add rice and continue to sauté until rice is light brown. Add broth and cinnamon stick.

Seal cooker and bring to high pressure quickly. Lower heat and cook for 25 minutes. Reduce pressure quickly under cold running water.

Season to taste, add raisins, remove cinnamon stick, and serve.

Indian Rice

This vibrant yellow dish is an exotic base for stir-fry vegetables or as a filling for pita pockets. It can also stand alone as a cold summer salad.

1	cup uncooked long grain brown rice	1	tablespoon minced fresh ginger
½	cup currants	1	teaspoon ground cardamom
½	cup Spanish peanuts	1	teaspoon turmeric

Add to pressure cooker rice, currants, peanuts, ginger, cardamom, turmeric, and 3 ¼ cups water. Seal cooker and bring to high pressure quickly. Lower heat and cook for 25 minutes. Let sit for 10 minutes, then reduce pressure quickly under cold running water. Simmer in open cooker if necessary to reduce liquid.

Tomato Rice Pilaf

SERVES 4

Brown rice contains the essential fatty acids, B vitamins, and fiber that white rice loses in refinement. For this reason, we have modified some popular Mediterranean dishes to include brown rice. We have used cilantro here but feel free to add whatever herbs you have in your refrigerator or garden. Green onions, chopped spinach leaves, Italian parsley, and chives would all be fine additions.

2	tablespoons extra virgin olive oil	1	can (28 ounces) whole peeled tomatoes, drained
1	medium yellow onion, chopped	1	cinnamon stick, about 3 inches long
4	cloves garlic, minced	1	tablespoon dried basil
1½	cups uncooked long grain brown rice	1	cup chopped fresh cilantro for garnish
2½	cups Vegetable Broth (page 108)		

Heat the olive oil in open pressure cooker over medium heat. Sauté onion, garlic, and rice until rice is light brown. Add broth, tomatoes, cinnamon, and basil.

Seal cooker and bring to high pressure quickly. Lower heat and cook for 30 minutes. Reduce pressure quickly under cold running water. Remove cinnamon stick. Garnish with cilantro and serve.

Kamut with Yogurt Sauce

SERVES 4

We love the look and flavor of this dish. The large kamut grains contrast in texture and appearance with the smaller spelt or wheat grains. If you cannot find kamut or spelt at your local health food store, you can order it through some of the mail-order sources in the appendix.

1   cup cooked kamut berries (pages 26–27)

1   cup cooked spelt or wheat berries (pages 26–27)

½   cup nonfat plain yogurt
    Dash of salt

1   tomato, seeded and chopped

1   avocado, peeled and chopped

Combine grain berries and cook or reheat. Meanwhile gently warm yogurt and salt in a small saucepan; do not let boil. Add tomato and heat for another minute, stirring gently. Remove from heat, gently stir in avocado, and serve over hot grains.

SOUPS

In this era of canned, instant, and dehydrated soups, who can resist the long-simmered taste of the real thing? The pressure cooker makes homemade soup a fast food. Always make more soup than you need for just one day: It tastes even better the second day. Soup also freezes well.

If any of these recipes exceed the volume of your cooker, cut the amount of water in half. This will give you a soup concentrate that requires less room for storage. The soup can be diluted to taste when reheating.

One of our favorite soup recipes is the ultimate winter warm-up: the soup sandwich. For those of you who have never been solaced by this treat, just pour a ladleful of any hot soup over thick slices of fresh bread. It is soft, warm, and comforting. Eat it with a spoon.

BROTH ENHANCERS

- Dry red wines such as Cabernet Sauvignon, Gamay Beaujolais, Merlot, Petite Sirah, Pinot Noir, Zinfandel, or a dry red wine blend are fabulous secret ingredients.
- Dry white wines such as Chardonnay, Sauvignon Blanc, or a dry white wine blend add a sweet zing to vegetable soups.
- A 6-inch strip of kombu (a sea vegetable) adds minerals, flavoring, and salt, enhancing other flavors in the soup.
- Canned vegetable broth can replace water, and dry bouillon can be added to water to flavor the grains and vegetables in the soup recipes.
- Bottled tomato juice added to cooking liquid makes a heartier soup.
- Fresh vegetable juices are a sneaky way to add more vegetables to soups.
- Freshly squeezed lemon or lime juice can make all the difference in flavoring. Lemon takes the edge off of strong-tasting vegetables, and lime adds an exotic South Pacific flavor to broth and soup.
- Nutritional yeast adds nutrients and a cheesy flavor to soups. Add 1 tablespoon per quart of liquid.
- Vinegars such as balsamic or red wine add tremendous flavor to broth.
- Miso paste or concentrate can be added after cooking for a salt alternative with an Asian flavor.
- Soy sauce or tamari can be added after cooking for more flavor.

NUTRITION TIPS FOR SOUPS

- If you want to lose weight, soup can help decrease your appetite. Just make sure the ingredients are lowfat.
- To reduce the fat in soups, do not add full-fat cream, cheese, or yogurt to the finished soup. Use nonfat yogurt (soy or dairy), lowfat sour cream, or soymilk.
- To make creamy lowfat soups, process all or part of the soup in a blender.
- Soup is a great over-the-counter medicine. Serve it hot to relieve stuffy sinuses. Light soups can provide your body with the liquids it needs during illness.
- Soup ingredients with medicinal value include garlic, onions, leeks, shiitake mushrooms, and ginger.

HOW TO THICKEN SOUPS

The thickness of soups can be varied by the amount of thickening agent you use. Always add thickeners after the soup has finished pressure cooking. Remove pan from heat, stir in thickening mixture, and return open pressure cooker to heat. Stir constantly until soup reaches desired thickness.

Flour 2 tablespoons whole wheat pastry flour to ¼ cup cold water. In a small bottle with lid (a small mayonnaise jar is perfect), shake flour and water until blended.

Arrowroot 1 tablespoon arrowroot to 2 tablespoons cold water. In a small cup, mix arrowroot and water together with a spoon.

Cornstarch 1 tablespoon cornstarch to 2 tablespoons cold water. In a small cup, mix cornstarch and water together with a spoon.

Bread crumbs ½ cup dried or 1 cup fresh bread crumbs to 4 cups soup.

Grated raw potatoes ½ to ⅔ cup grated raw potato to 4 cups soup. Heat for 15 minutes in open pan.

Vegetable Broth

This is where all your vegetable scraps should go. To flavor this broth, toss in peels, stems, green tops of leeks, celery leaves, wilted outer leaves, and so on of all your organic produce. Discard the peels of non-organic or waxed produce. This recipe makes a concentrated broth that can be diluted to suit your taste.

2	tablespoons extra virgin olive oil	2	tablespoons chopped fresh parsley
1	yellow onion, sliced	1/2	to 2 cups empty pea pods, potato peels, carrot peels, or other vegetable scraps
2	cloves garlic, minced		
1	carrot, sliced		
1	turnip, cut into 1-inch cubes	1	bay leaf
4	ribs celery with leaves, chopped	6	peppercorns
			Dried herbs of choice

Heat the olive oil in open pressure cooker over medium heat. Sauté onion, garlic, carrot, turnip, celery, parsley, and scraps for about 5 minutes. Add 3 cups water (or part water, part wine to make 3 cups liquid), bay leaf, peppercorns, and any dried seasonings you want.

Seal cooker and bring to high pressure slowly. Lower heat and cook for 10 minutes. Reduce pressure quickly under cold running water. Strain out the vegetables and save the broth.

To store, freeze concentrated broth in an ice cube tray. Transfer frozen cubes to thick plastic freezer bags to reduce the chance of freezer burn. Cubes can then be added to soup as necessary.

Golden Broth

This recipe can be used as a light broth or soup base. For a more concentrated broth, reduce the amount of water and dilute to taste when needed.

1 cup dried yellow, green, or pink lentils, picked over and rinsed

1 large yellow onion, chopped

4 cloves garlic, minced

2 tablespoons extra virgin olive oil

1 tablespoon turmeric

Add to pressure cooker lentils, onion, garlic, olive oil, turmeric, and 8 cups water. Seal cooker and bring to high pressure slowly. Lower heat and cook for 20 minutes. Reduce pressure quickly under cold running water.

Purée in blender if desired. Decrease water for a more concentrated broth.

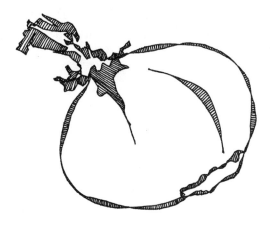

Miso Shiitake Broth

SERVES 6

This is a modified recipe from Goldie Caughlan that we have saved from our very first whole-foods class. This light broth is particularly nourishing when you are sick. The kombu, shiitake mushrooms, ginger juice, and miso all have medicinal benefits. For maximum taste and health benefits, add ginger juice and miso just before serving.

2 strips kombu, about
   8 inches long
3 to 4 dried shiitake
   mushrooms

2 teaspoons ginger juice
2 to 3 teaspoons miso
   Green onions, thinly sliced,
   for garnish

In open cooker, soak kombu and mushrooms in 6 cups water or vegetable broth for about 20 minutes. Remove when pliable and cut kombu into long 1-inch strips. Thinly slice across strips. Remove mushroom caps from stems, leave stems whole, and cut caps thinly. Return mushrooms and kombu to broth.

Seal cooker and bring to high pressure slowly. Lower heat and cook for 5 minutes. Reduce pressure quickly under cold running water or let fall on its own. Stir in ginger juice and miso. Garnish with green onions.

Grabure

This is the stout soup of Bearn, in southwest France.

7	cups Vegetable Broth (page 108)	1	large sweet potato, chopped into ½-inch slices
2	cups dried white beans such as cannellini, quick-soaked (page 28)	1	large white turnip, diced
		1	large yellow onion, quartered
1	can (8 ounces) water chestnuts, drained	1	head garlic, still attached to core and unpeeled (about 12 cloves)
½	small head red cabbage, chopped	1	tablespoon tamari or soy sauce
		½	teaspoon dried marjoram
½	cup green beans, cut into ½-inch lengths	½	teaspoon dried oregano
		¼	cup chopped fresh Italian parsley

Add to pressure cooker broth, white beans, water chestnuts, cabbage, green beans, sweet potato, turnip, onion, garlic, tamari, marjoram, and oregano.

Seal cooker and bring to high pressure slowly. Lower heat and cook for 20 minutes. Reduce pressure quickly under cold running water or let fall on its own. Remove garlic bulb. Stir in parsley and serve.

Winter Vegetable Soup

SERVES 10

A great way for the family to keep warm on those cold winter days. Just add some crusty warm bread to complete the meal.

2	tablespoons extra virgin olive oil	1	large russet potato, chopped
2	leeks, carefully cleaned and chopped	1/2	cup dried green split peas, picked over and rinsed
2	tablespoons minced garlic (about 9 cloves)	1/2	cup chopped fresh Italian parsley
6	cups Vegetable Broth (page 108)	1/2	cup coarsely chopped fresh basil leaves
6	medium carrots, sliced	2	teaspoons dried thyme
6	ripe plum tomatoes, seeded and cut into 1/2-inch cubes	1	teaspoon dried tarragon
1	small head red cabbage, chopped	1	tablespoon arrowroot dissolved in 1/4 cup water or broth

Heat the olive oil in open pressure cooker over medium heat. Sauté leeks and garlic until slightly browned. Add broth, carrots, tomatoes, cabbage, potato, split peas, parsley, basil, thyme, and tarragon.

Seal cooker and bring to high pressure slowly. Lower heat and cook for 15 minutes. Reduce pressure quickly under cold running water or let fall on its own. Stir in dissolved arrowroot and heat, stirring constantly, until soup reaches desired thickness.

Black and White Beans in Broth

SERVES 10

Add ¹/₄ cup mung bean sprouts to each bowl for a fresh flavor and crunchy texture. A lime wedge is the perfect garnish for this dish.

5	cups Vegetable Broth (page 108)	¹/₂	cup snow peas
1	cup dried cannellini beans, quick-soaked (page 28)	2	tablespoons soy sauce
1	cup dried black beans, quick-soaked (page 28)	2	tablespoons sherry
1	rib celery, chopped	1	tablespoon minced fresh ginger
1	leek, carefully cleaned and sliced into rounds	1	teaspoon hot chile paste
1	large carrot, chopped	2	cloves garlic, minced
		¹/₂	cup chopped fresh Italian parsley

Add to pressure cooker broth, cannellini beans, black beans, celery, leek, carrot, snow peas, soy sauce, sherry, ginger, chile paste, garlic, and parsley. Seal cooker and bring to high pressure slowly. Lower heat and cook for 20 minutes. Reduce pressure quickly under cold running water or let fall on its own.

Asian Bean Sprout Soup

SERVES 4

The marinade infuses the tofu with a variety of rich flavors.

½	block (½ pound) reduced-fat firm tofu, cut into 1-inch cubes	6	cups Vegetable Broth (page 108)
2	tablespoons soy sauce or tamari	1	large yellow onion, sliced
2	tablespoons minced garlic	1	large carrot, peeled and cut in thin strips
1	tablespoon minced fresh ginger	1	cup shredded bok choy
1	tablespoon freshly squeezed lemon juice	3	green onions, sliced
1	tablespoon balsamic vinegar	2	tablespoons sesame seeds
		1	cup mung bean sprouts for garnish

In open pressure cooker off heat, marinate tofu in soy sauce, garlic, ginger, lemon juice, and vinegar for 20 minutes. Add broth, onion, carrot, bok choy, green onions, and sesame seeds.

Seal cooker and bring to high pressure quickly. Lower heat and cook for 5 minutes. Reduce pressure quickly under cold running water or let fall on its own. Ladle soup into serving bowls and garnish each with a handful of mung bean sprouts.

Indonesian Root Vegetable Soup with Coconut Milk

SERVES 6

This Thai soup is the perfect blend of creamy and spicy. It is a meal on its own.

3	tablespoons extra virgin olive oil	3	cups Vegetable Broth (page 108)
2	yellow onions, sliced	3	medium new red potatoes, diced
3	shallots, minced	1	rutabaga, diced
4	cloves garlic, minced	1	turnip, diced
1	Anaheim chile pepper, finely chopped	1	parsnip, diced
2	teaspoons grated fresh ginger	2	cups sliced button mushrooms
2	tablespoons curry powder	1	can (about 16 ounces) reduced-fat coconut milk
1	teaspoon ground cumin		Juice of 1 lime
1	teaspoon turmeric		

Heat the olive oil in open pressure cooker over medium heat. Sauté onions, shallots, garlic, chile, ginger, curry powder, cumin, and turmeric until onions are translucent. Add broth, potatoes, rutabaga, turnip, and parsnip.

Seal cooker and bring to high pressure slowly. Lower heat and cook for 5 minutes. Reduce pressure quickly under cold running water. Stir in mushrooms and coconut milk, and lime juice to taste.

Mexican Tortilla Soup

SERVES 10

This spicy south-of-the-border soup can be made with fresh chiles or ground dried New Mexico or California chiles.

1	tablespoon extra virgin olive oil	7 1/2	cups Vegetable Broth (page 108)
4	yellow onions, thinly sliced	1/4	cup flour
1	tablespoon chopped garlic		
3	tablespoons ground dried New Mexico or California chiles (recipe follows)		**Garnish**
		1	cup shredded Monterey Jack cheese with jalapeño chiles
1	teaspoon ground cumin	1/2	cup chopped fresh cilantro
1	teaspoon dried oregano		Fried tortilla strips (recipe follows)

Heat the olive oil in open pressure cooker over medium heat. Sauté onions, garlic, chiles, cumin, and oregano for about 5 minutes. Add 2 cups of the broth.

Seal cooker and bring to high pressure quickly. Lower heat and cook for 5 minutes. Reduce pressure quickly under cold running water.

Return open cooker to high heat and scrape free the caramelized onions from bottom of pan. Dissolve flour in 1 cup of the broth. Add flour mixture and remaining broth to cooker and cook, stirring, until soup has thickened. Ladle into bowls and sprinkle with cheese, cilantro, and tortilla strips.

GROUND DRIED CHILE PEPPERS

Grind dried chile pepper to a fine powder in blender, coffee grinder, or pestle and mortar. Store in airtight container in refrigerator or freezer.

Be careful when working with the chiles. Wear kitchen gloves, do not touch eyes or mouth, and after preparation wash gloves and hands thoroughly with soap and water.

FRIED TORTILLA STRIPS

1	tablespoon extra virgin olive oil	6	corn tortillas, cut into 4-inch slices
¼	teaspoon chile flakes		

Heat olive oil and chile flakes over high heat in sauté pan. Add tortilla strips and fry until crisp and golden.

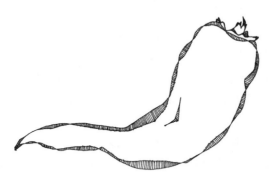

West Indian Squash Soup

SERVES 8

Any seasonal squash will work well in this recipe but pumpkin and butternut are exceptionally rich and delicious. Serve with a dollop of lowfat sour cream or nonfat yogurt, and freshly ground nutmeg.

2	tablespoons extra virgin olive oil	2	cups peeled and cubed butternut squash
1	red onion, diced	2	Anaheim chile peppers
1	yellow onion, diced	1	mild red chile pepper, such as ancho
3	cloves garlic, minced		Yogurt (soy or dairy) or sour cream for garnish
6	cups Vegetable Broth (page 108)		
2	cups uncooked short grain brown rice	1	tablespoon freshly ground nutmeg for garnish

Heat the olive oil in open pressure cooker over medium heat. Sauté both onions and garlic until browning begins. Add broth, rice, squash, Anaheim chiles, and red chile.

Seal cooker and bring to high pressure slowly. Lower heat and cook for 25 minutes. Reduce pressure quickly under cold running water or let fall on its own.

Serve in bowls topped with a dollop of yogurt or sour cream and a sprinkle of ground nutmeg.

Spicy Lentil Soup

The North African influence in this old Sephardic Jewish recipe is evident when you taste its rich aromatic spice combination. For a saltier version, add soy sauce and a splash of freshly squeezed lemon juice.

1 tablespoon extra virgin olive oil	1 cup dried green or brown lentils, picked over and rinsed
1 large yellow onion, quartered	1 cup dried red lentils, picked over and rinsed
6 cloves garlic, minced	
1 large carrot, sliced	2 bay leaves
1 rib celery, sliced	1 teaspoon ground cumin
1 can (28 ounces) whole peeled tomatoes with juice, chopped	1 teaspoon ground allspice
	1 teaspoon ground cinnamon
5 cups Vegetable Broth (page 108)	1 pinch saffron threads (about 10 threads)

Heat the olive oil in open pressure cooker over medium heat. Sauté onions and garlic until slightly browned. Add carrot, celery, tomatoes, broth, green lentils, red lentils, bay leaves, cumin, allspice, cinnamon, and saffron.

Seal cooker and bring to high pressure over medium heat. Lower heat and cook for 15 minutes. Reduce pressure quickly under cold running water or let fall on its own. Remove bay leaves before serving.

Mint Pea Soup

SERVES 10

3	tablespoons extra virgin olive oil	1	package (10 ounces) frozen spinach
2	yellow onions, diced	1/2	cup white wine
2	tablespoons minced garlic	1/4	cup chopped fresh mint
2	packages (10 ounces each) frozen peas	1	bunch cilantro, stemmed
		2	tablespoons ground cumin
			Juice of 1 lemon

Heat the olive oil in open pressure cooker over medium heat. Sauté onions and garlic until translucent. Add peas, spinach, and 8 cups water.

Seal cooker and bring to high pressure slowly. Lower heat and cook for 3 minutes. Reduce pressure quickly under cold running water.

Add wine, mint, and cilantro. Cook in open pressure cooker for 5 minutes. Purée mixture in blender 2 cups at a time to avoid overflow. Return purée to cooker and stir in cumin and lemon juice.

Creamy Carrot Soup

SERVES 10

2	tablespoons extra virgin olive oil		2	yams, peeled and chopped
1	large yellow onion, chopped		2	tablespoons chopped fresh mint leaves
3	tablespoons grated fresh ginger		1/2	cup white wine
8	medium carrots, peeled and chopped			Juice of 1 lemon
				Juice of 1 orange
			1	tablespoon Dijon mustard

Heat the olive oil in open pressure cooker over medium heat. Sauté onions until translucent. Add ginger and continue sautéing for 1 minute. Add carrots, yams, and 8 cups water.

Seal cooker and bring to high pressure slowly. Lower heat and cook for 5 minutes. Reduce pressure quickly under cold running water.

Return open cooker to medium heat, add mint, and simmer for 10 minutes. Purée in blender, 2 cups at a time to avoid overflow. Pour purée back into cooker and add wine, lemon juice, orange juice, and mustard. Whisk thoroughly and serve warm.

Creamy Potato-Onion Soup

SERVES 8

For a creamy texture process all or part of the soup in a blender until smooth.

4   red potatoes, peeled and
    chopped
4   yellow onions, chopped
4   cups Vegetable Broth
    (page 108)

1   cup milk (soy, dairy, or goat)
1   teaspoon salt
1   teaspoon ground
    white pepper

Add potatoes, onions, and broth to pressure cooker. Seal cooker and bring to high pressure slowly. Lower heat and cook for 10 minutes. Reduce pressure quickly under cold running water.

Stir in milk. Add salt and pepper to taste and serve.

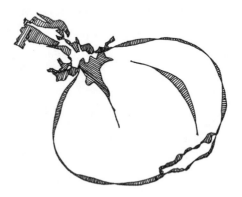

Lemon Vegetable Soup

SERVES 8

This subtle blend of lemon and mint with just a hint of garlic is a light, fresh, summer soup. Garnish with freshly ground black pepper and a lemon wedge.

4	cups Vegetable Broth (page 108)	2	plum tomatoes, peeled, seeded, and chopped
1	large yellow onion, diced	1/2	cup chopped fresh dill
4	cloves garlic, minced	1/2	cup chopped fresh Italian parsley
1	large carrot, diced		
1	large parsnip, diced	3	tablespoons freshly squeezed lemon juice
1	large rib celery, diced		
		1/4	cup chopped fresh mint

Add to pressure cooker broth, onion, garlic, carrot, parsnip, celery, tomatoes, dill, and parsley. Seal cooker and bring to high pressure slowly. Lower heat and cook for 10 minutes. Reduce pressure quickly under cold running water or let fall on its own. Stir in lemon juice and mint and serve.

Cannellini Soup with Pistou

SERVES 10

Pistou is the French version of pesto. Homemade pistou is so much more flavorful than commercial preparations. However, if time or energy is in short supply, a store-bought version can be used. The Parmesan cheese can easily be left out if you are vegan.

6	cups Vegetable Broth (page 108)	2	cups dried cannelini beans, presoaked (page 28)
1	yellow onion, chopped	1	can (15 ounces) whole peeled tomatoes, drained and seeded
3	cloves garlic, minced		
1	fennel bulb, diced		
1	red potato, diced	2	tablespoons sherry
1	rib celery, diced	1	tablespoon dried basil
1	carrot, diced	2	bay leaves
1	zucchini, diced	10	tablespoons pistou (recipe below)

Add to pressure cooker broth, onion, garlic, fennel, potato, celery, carrot, zucchini, cannellini beans, tomatoes, sherry, basil, and bay leaves. Seal cooker and bring to high pressure slowly. Lower heat and cook for 15 minutes. Reduce pressure quickly under cold running water or let fall on its own.

Remove bay leaves. Ladle soup into bowls and garnish each with 1 tablespoon of pistou.

PISTOU ·

½ cup fresh basil leaves	2 tablespoons extra virgin olive oil
2 cloves garlic	
¼ cup grated Parmesan cheese	2 tablespoons Vegetable Broth (page 108)

Combine basil, garlic, Parmesan, olive oil, and broth in a food processor. Pulse for 15 seconds or until mixture is well blended. Makes 10 tablespoons.

To store pistou in refrigerator, pour a thin layer of olive oil over the top. The pistou can be used as a flavor-enhancer in clear broth soups.

Greek Tomato Soup (Domatosoupa)

SERVES 6

This may be the most flavorful tomato soup you will ever have. The rich combination of spices make a warming conglomeration of flavors.

3	tablespoons extra virgin olive oil	1/4	cup sun-dried tomatoes, chopped, or 2 tablespoons sun-dried tomato paste
1	large yellow onion, chopped		
2	cloves garlic, minced (about 1 teaspoon)	1	small hot green chile pepper, such as kenyan, sliced thin
1	leek, carefully cleaned and chopped	1/2	cup chopped fresh Italian parsley
1	can (28 ounces) stewed tomatoes with juice, chopped	2	teaspoons finely chopped fresh mint
		1 1/2	cups sour cream or yogurt (made from soymilk or dairy)

Heat the olive oil in open pressure cooker over medium heat. Sauté onion, garlic, and leek until onion softens. Add stewed tomatoes, sun-dried tomatoes, chile, parsley, mint, and 1 cup water.

Seal cooker and bring to high pressure slowly. Lower heat and cook for 5 minutes. Reduce pressure quickly under cold running water. Mix in sour cream and serve.

Variation *Any combination of the following ingredients can be used in this soup. Remove hard items like bay leaves, cloves, and cinnamon sticks before serving.*

2	tablespoons fresh thyme	2	strips lemon zest
2	tablespoons fresh marjoram	1	whole clove
1	tablespoon dried oregano	1	small cinnamon stick
1	teaspoon sugar		Salt and freshly ground
2	bay leaves		black pepper

Borscht

SERVES 6

This recipe uses the whole beet, root and greens, maximizing the nutrient content of this delicious soup.

2	tablespoons extra virgin olive oil	½	head green cabbage, sliced thin
1	small yellow onion, diced	1	potato, sliced thin
3	cloves garlic, minced	1	carrot, sliced thin
5	cups Vegetable Broth (page 108)	1	rib celery, sliced thin
1	bunch beets with greens, sliced thin and greens shredded or 2 cans (8 ounces each) sliced beets	2	tablespoons tomato paste
		1	teaspoon honey
		2	tablespoons whole wheat flour dissolved in ¼ cup water

Heat the olive oil in open pressure cooker over medium heat. Sauté onion and garlic until translucent. Stir in broth, beets with greens, cabbage, potato, carrot, celery, tomato paste, and honey. Make sure paste and honey dissolve; if they fall in clumps to the bottom of the cooker they may scorch.

Seal cooker and bring to high pressure slowly. Lower heat and cook for 20 minutes. Reduce pressure quickly under cold running water. Return open cooker to heat and stir in flour mixture. Heat, stirring constantly, until soup has reached desired thickness.

Hearty Potato-Leek Soup

SERVES 6

For a creamier soup, purée all or part of the recipe before adding the milk.

2	tablespoons extra virgin olive oil	1	tablespoon tamari or soy sauce
1	large yellow onion, chopped	1	tablespoon chopped fresh thyme
2	large leeks, carefully cleaned and chopped	1	bay leaf
4	cups Vegetable Broth (page 108)	1/2	cup soymilk or condensed lowfat milk
5	large ribs celery, diced		Salt and freshly ground black pepper
4	large russet potatoes, diced		

Heat the olive oil in open pressure cooker over medium heat. Sauté onion and leeks for several minutes until onion is translucent. Add broth, celery, potatoes, tamari, thyme, and bay leaf.

Seal cooker and bring to high pressure slowly. Lower heat and cook for 5 minutes. Reduce pressure quickly under cold running water or let fall on its own.

Remove bay leaf and return open cooker to heat. Add milk, stirring gently to heat. Season with salt and pepper to taste.

Garlicky Ginger Soup with Basmati Rice

SERVES 8

A recipe for garlic lovers. Sprinkle each serving with shredded coconut for an unusual presentation.

2	tablespoons extra virgin olive oil	4	cups Vegetable Broth (page 108)
2	large yellow onions, diced	1½	cups uncooked basmati rice
12	cloves garlic, minced	2	carrots, sliced
2	tablespoons minced fresh ginger	½	cup currants
1	red bell pepper, seeded and diced	2	whole cloves
		1	cinnamon stick, 8 to 10 inches long

Heat the olive oil in open pressure cooker over medium heat. Sauté onions, garlic, ginger, and red pepper until onions brown. Add broth, rice, carrots, currants, cloves, and cinnamon stick.

Seal cooker and bring to high pressure quickly. Lower heat and cook for 25 minutes. Reduce pressure quickly under cold running water or let fall on its own. Remove cloves and cinnamon stick before serving.

9

SALADS

Hot-weather salads are easy to make. Toss leftover grains, beans, or vegetables with one of the dressings below and serve on a bed of shredded carrots or in lettuce cups. A slice or two of fresh whole grain bread completes the menu for an easy lunch or light supper.

Instructions and timetables for cooking plain grains, legumes, and vegetables can be found in chapter 3.

Salad Dressings

BASIC CREAM DRESSING
MAKES ABOUT 1¼ CUPS

By adding fresh herbs, you can vary the flavor of this dressing to suit your mood and taste buds.

6   ounces reduced-fiber smooth tofu, drained and well squeezed

2   tablespoons freshly squeezed lemon juice (or frozen if fresh is not available)

2   tablespoons canola oil

2   tablespoons white, mellow, or yellow miso

2   teaspoons dried herbs such as oregano, parsley, or thyme

Combine tofu, lemon juice, oil, miso, and herbs in blender or food processor. Blend until smooth.

BASIC VINEGAR AND OIL DRESSING
MAKES ABOUT 1 CUP

½   cup extra virgin olive oil

¼   cup cold freshly squeezed lemon juice (or frozen if fresh is not available)

¼   cup cold balsamic vinegar

2   tablespoons cold tamari

Place olive oil, lemon juice, vinegar, and tamari into a jar. Screw top on securely and shake well.

BASIC YOGURT HERB DRESSING
MAKES ABOUT 1 CUP

For this recipe you can use soy, goat's, or cow's yogurt. For a really unusual treat, substitute flavored yogurt for all or part of the plain yogurt.

1 cup nonfat plain yogurt	3/4 teaspoon fresh dill or 1/4 teaspoon dried dill (or other herb)
1 tablespoon chopped green onion	
3/4 teaspoon dried parsley	1/4 teaspoon celery salt Dash of salt

Combine yogurt, green onion, parsley, dill, celery salt, and salt and chill. If dressing is too thick, thin with 1 tablespoon milk.

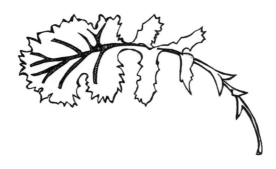

Salads

Warm Jerusalem Artichoke Salad

SERVES 4

Jerusalem artichokes are crunchy tubers with the flavor of a globe artichoke. They are not commonly used in the U.S., yet are now widely available. You can impress your guests with this still-unusual vegetable.

6	Jerusalem artichokes, peeled and halved
3	carrots, peeled and halved lengthwise
¼	cup chopped Italian parsley
1	head romaine lettuce

Dressing

¼	cup extra virgin olive oil
2	tablespoons balsamic vinegar
1	tablespoon Dijon mustard
1	teaspoon honey

Add artichokes and 2 cups water to pressure cooker. Seal cooker and bring to high pressure quickly. Lower heat and cook for 5 minutes. Reduce pressure quickly under cold running water. Slice artichokes and carrots into thin strips.

To make dressing, whisk together olive oil, vinegar, mustard, and honey. Toss vegetables with dressing and parsley and serve over a bed of romaine lettuce.

Wilted Garlic Greens and Pine Nut Salad

SERVES 4

Flash-cooking these nutrient powerhouses makes the greens more digestible. The sea salt in the dressing adds flavor and healthful minerals.

2	cups shredded bok choy	**Dressing**
1	cup shredded mustard greens	¼ cup pine nuts
1	cup shredded kale	¼ cup extra virgin olive oil
6	cloves garlic, minced	Juice of ½ lemon
		Salt to taste

Add bok choy, mustard greens, kale, garlic, and 2 cups water to pressure cooker. Seal cooker and bring to high pressure quickly. Lower heat and cook for 2 minutes. Reduce pressure quickly under cold running water.

To make dressing, combine pine nuts, olive oil, lemon juice, and salt. Toss with vegetables.

Broccoli and Blue Cheese Salad

SERVES 4 TO 6

Rich blue cheese, a fresh splash of orange juice, and balsamic vinegar make this the perfect salad from picnic table to formal table.

2	medium heads broccoli, cut into florets
1/2	red onion, finely chopped
4	ounces blue cheese, crumbled

Dressing

3	tablespoons extra virgin olive oil
6	tablespoons balsamic vinegar
2	cloves garlic, minced
	Juice of 1 orange
	Chopped fresh basil, optional

Special Equipment

Trivet

Pour 2 cups water into pressure cooker and place trivet inside. Set broccoli florets on trivet. Seal cooker and bring to high pressure quickly. Lower heat and cook for 2 minutes. Reduce pressure quickly under cold running water, and cool broccoli in ice water. Strain and set aside.

To make dressing, in a large bowl whisk together olive oil, vinegar, garlic, orange juice, and basil. Add broccoli, red onion, and blue cheese crumbles. Toss and serve.

Tangy Potato Salad

SERVES 6

Balsamic vinegar gives a new twist to this old favorite.

5	medium russet potatoes, chopped
1	red onion, chopped
3	green onions, chopped
1	cup diced celery

Dressing

3	tablespoons extra virgin olive oil
3	tablespoons balsamic vinegar
	Juice of 1/2 orange
2	tablespoons mayonnaise
2	teaspoons Dijon-style mustard
1	tablespoon minced garlic
1/2	tablespoon dried oregano

Add potatoes and 4 cups water to pressure cooker. Seal cooker and bring to high pressure quickly. Lower heat and cook for 5 minutes. Reduce pressure quickly under cold running water.

Drain water and place potatoes in the refrigerator immediately. Leave potatoes to chill for 10 minutes while preparing dressing.

In a large bowl, combine olive oil, vinegar, orange juice, mayonnaise, mustard, garlic, and oregano. Add chilled potatoes, red and green onions, and celery. Toss and serve.

Curry Lentil Salad

If you can't find dried cranberries (sometimes called craisins), sub-stitute sultanas. Sultanas are dried grapes that are sweeter than cur-rants and not as acidic as raisins.

2	cups nonfat plain yogurt	2	cups cooked lentils (pages 28–29)
1	tablespoon freshly squeezed lime juice (or frozen if fresh is not available)	3/4	cup dried cranberries
		1/2	cup fresh or frozen peas
2	teaspoons honey	1/2	cup toasted sliced almonds
2	teaspoons curry powder	3	green onions, chopped (about 1/4 cup)
1/4	teaspoon ground cinnamon		
1/4	teaspoon ground ginger		

In a large bowl combine yogurt, lime juice, honey, curry powder, cin-namon, and ginger and mix well. Add lentils, cranberries, peas, almonds, and green onions. Serve chilled.

Black Bean and Cheese Salad

This salad is based on a recipe we adapted from one of our favorite cookbooks, Nikki and David Goldbeck's American Wholefoods Cuisine. *This recipe calls for black beans but any bean can be used.*

4	ounces cheddar cheese, grated	2	green onions, chopped
1	cup nonfat yogurt	2	cups grated carrots
1	tablespoon freshly squeezed lemon juice (or frozen if fresh is not available)	2	cups shredded lettuce
		4	large tomatoes
½	teaspoon prepared mustard	2	cups cooked black beans (pages 28–29)

In a food processor, purée cheese, yogurt, lemon juice, mustard, and green onions until sauce is smooth. Set aside.

Combine carrots and lettuce, and divide among 4 plates. Cut each tomato into quarters, stopping ½ inch from the base so that slices are attached. Set a tomato on top of each plate of shredded vegetables.

In a bowl, combine cheese sauce with black beans. Spoon black bean mixture into tomatoes.

Three-Bean Picnic Salad

SERVES 8

This recipe contains no eggs or mayonnaise to spoil, making it perfect for your next family picnic or potluck. Make the salad the day before and let it marinate in the refrigerator overnight.

2 cups minced fresh Italian parsley	1 cup cooked red kidney beans (pages 28–29)
1 cup extra virgin olive oil	1 cup cooked small white beans (pages 28–29)
1/4 freshly squeezed lemon juice (or frozen if fresh is not available)	1 cup cooked chickpeas (pages 28–29)
4 cloves garlic, minced (about 2 teaspoons)	1 cup chopped raw broccoli
Salt to taste	1 large red onion, thinly sliced

In a jar combine parsley, olive oil, lemon juice, garlic, and salt and shake well. Toss kidney beans, white beans, chickpeas, broccoli, and red onion with dressing. Let it sit covered in refrigerator until well chilled.

Chickpea Salad

Serve this salad on large lettuce leaves. This high-protein meal will give you long-lasting energy. Great for active days.

1	cup nonfat yogurt (or 4 ounces silken tofu)	1/8	teaspoon turmeric
2	teaspoons freshly squeezed lemon juice (or frozen if fresh is not available)	2	cups cooked chickpeas, cooled (pages 28–29)
		1/2	cup halved button mushrooms
		1/2	cup sliced Greek olives
1	clove garlic, minced	1/2	cup minced yellow onion
1/2	teaspoon ground cumin	2	medium tomatoes, chopped

In a large bowl combine yogurt, lemon juice, garlic, cumin, and turmeric and mix well. Add chickpeas, mushrooms, olives, onion, and tomatoes. Toss until thoroughly coated with yogurt mixture.

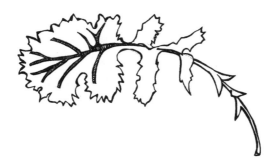

Salads

Spicy White Bean Salad

The lemon zest and mint make this salad especially refreshing.

Grated zest and juice of ¹/₂ lemon
1 tablespoon extra virgin olive oil
2 cloves garlic, minced
2 teaspoons Dijon mustard
1 teaspoon honey

2 cups cooked white beans (pages 28–29)
1 cup carrot curls
2 plum tomatoes, chopped
1 medium yellow onion, diced
2 tablespoons chopped fresh mint

In a bowl combine lemon zest and juice, olive oil, garlic, mustard, and honey. Mix well. Add white beans, carrots, tomatoes, onion, and mint and toss. Serve chilled.

Mexicali Salad

This zesty recipe can be served warm or chilled. Serve with toasted pita bread or tortillas topped with melted sharp cheddar cheese.

¼   cup red wine vinegar or
    balsamic vinegar

2   tablespoons freshly squeezed
    lime juice (or frozen if fresh
    is not available)

2   tablespoons honey

1   teaspoon ground cumin

½   cup minced fresh cilantro

1   cup cooked black beans
    (pages 28–29)

1   cup cooked wild rice
    (pages 28–29)

1   package (14 ounces) frozen
    corn, thawed

2   tomatoes, diced

1   red bell pepper, seeded and
    chopped

1   cup chopped green onions

In a large bowl combine vinegar, lime juice, honey, cumin, and cilantro and whisk until well mixed. Add black beans, rice, corn, tomatoes, red pepper, and green onions and toss well. Chill in refrigerator for at least 1 hour.

Barley and Kidney Bean Salad

Serves 4 to 6

Barley offers a nice change of pace from rice in this salad flavored by a nonfat honey-mustard dressing. If a richer dressing is desired, add 1 tablespoon extra virgin olive oil along with the vinegar and mustard.

2 tablespoons balsamic vinegar	1 cup cooked kidney beans (pages 28–29)
2 tablespoons Dijon mustard	
2 tablespoons honey	1 medium tomato, chopped
2 teaspoons grated fresh ginger	½ cup chopped celery
½ teaspoon freshly ground black pepper	½ cup chopped green pepper
1 cup cooked barley (pages 26–27)	½ cup chopped red onion

In a bowl combine vinegar, mustard, honey, ginger, and black pepper and whisk until well mixed. Add barley, kidney beans, tomato, celery, green pepper, and red onion and toss. Chill in refrigerator for at least 1 hour.

Warm Garbanzo Bean Salad

Serve this salad with hot soup and crusty warm bread for a cold-weather lunch.

2	cups dried garbanzo beans, presoaked (page 28)	1	teaspoon paprika
1	can (28 ounces) whole peeled tomatoes, drained and chopped	1/2	teaspoon ground coriander
		1/2	cup chopped fresh cilantro
1/2	cup sliced green onions	2	tablespoons freshly squeezed lemon juice (or frozen if fresh is not available)
1	teaspoon ground cumin	1/2	teaspoon salt

Add beans, tomatoes, green onions, cumin, paprika, and coriander to pressure cooker. Seal cooker and bring to high pressure quickly. Lower heat and cook for 20 minutes. Reduce pressure quickly under cold running water. Stir in cilantro, lemon juice, and salt. Serve warm.

Brown Rice Salad

Serves 8

Cold brown rice salad is the perfect packable lunch to take to work, picnics, or on the road.

1	tablespoon extra virgin olive oil	1	teaspoon dried dill
1	teaspoon chopped garlic	2	cups seeded thin strips tomato
1	cup uncooked medium or long grain brown rice	1	cup thinly sliced red bell pepper
3	tablespoons white wine vinegar	10	Greek olives, pitted and halved

Heat the olive oil in open pressure cooker over medium heat. Sauté garlic until soft. Add rice, 3 cups water, vinegar, and dill to cooker.

Seal cooker and bring to high pressure quickly. Lower heat and cook for 25 minutes. Reduce pressure quickly under cold running water. Gently stir in tomato, red pepper, and olives. Serve warm or chilled.

Wild Rice and Apple Salad with Mint

SERVES 6

Serve this salad over a bed of baby spinach leaves.

½	cup orange juice	3	cups cooked brown rice (pages 26–27)
½	cup chopped fresh mint		
¼	cup honey	3	cups cooked wild rice (pages 26–27)
	Juice of 1 lime		
½	teaspoon coarsely ground black pepper	1	large Granny Smith apple, diced

In a bowl combine orange juice, mint, honey, lime juice, and black pepper. Add brown rice, wild rice, and apple and toss. Serve cold.

Greek Bulgur Salad

Fresh feta cheese comes in strong and mild varieties. It can be purchased at most grocery stores, almost all delis, and some health food stores.

1	cup cooked bulgur (pages 26–27)	2	tablespoons extra virgin olive oil
½	cup diced tomatoes	2	tablespoons freshly squeezed lemon juice (or frozen if fresh is not available)
½	cup chopped fresh parsley		
¼	cup crumbled fresh feta cheese	2	tablespoons dried mint
¼	cup pine nuts	1	tablespoon fresh or dried thyme

In a large bowl combine bulgur, tomatoes, parsley, feta, pine nuts, olive oil, lemon juice, mint, and thyme. Toss gently and serve.

Asian Salsa and Quinoa

SERVES 2

Serve with a side of julienned cucumbers which are cooling and delicious with this salad.

3   large tomatoes, seeded and diced
2   green onions, minced
¼   cup minced fresh cilantro
1   teaspoon sesame oil

1   teaspoon soy sauce or tamari
½   teaspoon hot chile oil
2   cups cooked quinoa, cooled (pages 26–27)

Combine tomatoes, green onions, cilantro, sesame oil, soy sauce, and chile oil and mix well. Add quinoa, toss lightly, and serve.

Salads

Raspberry Amaranth Salad

SERVES 4

Amaranth was a staple food of the Aztecs. Its seed is very small, about the size of a grain of sand. It has a delightful woodsy flavor. We use it here on a light salad that goes well with a hearty casserole.

½	cup raspberry vinegar	1	cup cooked dry-roasted amaranth (pages 26–27)
2	tablespoons freshly squeezed lemon juice (or frozen if fresh is not available)	4	cups salad greens, divided among 4 plates
2	tablespoons soy sauce	1	cup fresh raspberries
1	tablespoon walnut oil (or olive, canola, or high-oleic safflower oil)		

In a bowl combine vinegar, lemon juice, soy sauce, and oil and whisk until well mixed. Add amaranth and continue to whisk. Pour immediately over greens and sprinkle each salad with ¼ cup berries.

Asian Greens and Quinoa

SERVES 4

Use a combination of Asian greens and Brassica family vegetables such as mustard greens, Chinese cabbage, kale, brussels sprouts, savoy or red cabbage, cauliflower, broccoli, and kohlrabi mixed with quinoa for a warm dish or chill for a cold salad.

1 tablespoon extra virgin olive oil	1 cup Vegetable Broth (page 108)
3 cups shredded bok choy	2 cups cooked quinoa (pages 26–27)
3 tablespoons sesame seeds	
2 tablespoons soy sauce	

Heat the olive oil in open pressure cooker or sauté pan over medium heat. Sauté bok choy, sesame seeds, and soy sauce. Add vegetable broth.

Seal cooker and bring to high pressure quickly. Lower heat and cook for 1 minute. Reduce pressure quickly under cold running water. Spoon mixture over the quinoa and serve.

10

STUFFINGS, SPREADS, AND DIPS

Your pressure cooker can be used creatively to make healthful stuffings, spreads, and dips. Appetizers that were once too time-consuming for the average working person can now be made simply and quickly with a pressure cooker.

We have developed numerous recipes with an international influence to bring you adaptations of favorite bean, vegetable, and grain dishes for the pressure cooker. By including high-fiber and protein-rich beans, vitamin- and fiber-rich grains as well as vitamin- and mineral-packed vegetables, we have ensured that these recipes not only taste decadent but are also good for you.

Instructions and timetables for cooking legumes, grains, and vegetables can be found in chapter 3.

GOOD FOODS TO COVER WITH SPREADS

chipatis (flat whole grain
    bread)
flat bread
flour and corn tortillas
pita pockets
raw vegetable slices

sliced whole grain breads
taco shells
wasa bread or rye tac
whole grain bagels
whole grain crackers

GOOD VEGETABLES TO STUFF

bell peppers
cabbage and bok choy
    leaves
grape leaves
large mushroom caps

mini pumpkins
onions
summer and winter squash
tomatoes
zucchini

GOOD FOODS TO DIP

artichokes
bread sticks
crackers
mini rice cakes
pieces of fruit
pretzels

strips of toasted
    pita pockets
strips of warm focaccia
    or chipatis
taco chips
vegetable sticks

Onions Stuffed
with Cheese

SERVES 4

The custard cups help the onions to keep their shape while cooking.

4	very large sweet onions	1	medium tomato, minced
2	cups grated sharp cheddar cheese	⅛	teaspoon freshly ground black pepper
1½	cups cooked long grain brown rice (pages 26–27)		Finely ground bread crumbs

Special Equipment
Trivet
Four 10-ounce custard dishes
Cover for onions (wax paper or foil)

To hollow onions, peel and cut off the bottoms so they stand on their own. With a knife and spoon, scoop out all but the outer two or three rings. Refrigerate the onion "innards" for use in another dish.

In a bowl combine cheese, rice, tomato, and black pepper. Gently press stuffing into onions until they are three-quarters full. Place 1 stuffed onion into each custard dish and cover to protect from condensation.

Pour 1 cup water into pressure cooker and place trivet inside. Place custard dishes on trivet. Seal cooker and bring to high pressure quickly. Lower heat and cook for 6 minutes. Reduce pressure quickly under cold running water. Dust tops of onions with bread crumbs.

Mushroom-Stuffed Peppers

SERVES 4

Make sure that you purchase peppers with flat bottoms so that they will stand up in the cooker. Use this stuffing in onions, tomatoes, or squash for variety.

2	tablespoons extra virgin olive oil	1	tablespoon chopped fresh thyme
2	tablespoons minced yellow onions	2	tablespoons grated Parmesan cheese
½	cup chopped mushrooms	4	green bell peppers, topped and seeded
¼	cup chopped tomatoes		
2	tablespoons minced Italian parsley		

Special Equipment
Trivet, sprayed with vegetable oil
Cover for bell peppers (wax paper or foil)
Tongs

Heat the olive oil in open pressure cooker over medium heat. Sauté onions, mushrooms, tomatoes, parsley, and thyme. Add Parmesan and mix well. Stuff the bell peppers with the mixture.

Pour 1 cup water into pressure cooker and place trivet inside. Place stuffed peppers on trivet, being careful that peppers do not touch the sides of the cooker. Cover peppers to protect from condensation.

Seal cooker and bring to high pressure quickly. Lower heat and cook for 4 minutes. Reduce pressure quickly under cold running water, taking care that the cooker does not slant and topple the peppers. Carefully remove peppers from cooker with tongs.

Stuffings, Spreads, and Dips

Millet-Stuffed Tomatoes

SERVES 4

A wonderful main course to serve alone for a light lunch or with a green salad for dinner.

1	tablespoon extra virgin olive oil	½	teaspoon dried marjoram
1	medium yellow onion, diced	½	teaspoon dried oregano
3	cloves garlic, minced	¼	teaspoon dried thyme
3	cups cooked millet (pages 26–27)		Freshly ground black pepper to taste
1	cooking apple, cored and diced		Vegetable Broth as needed (page 108)
2	tablespoons minced fresh parsley	4	tomatoes, topped and seeded

Special Equipment
Trivet, sprayed with vegetable oil
Cover for tomatoes (wax paper or foil)
Tongs

Heat the olive oil in open pressure cooker over medium heat. Sauté onion and garlic until soft. In a large bowl combine onion mixture, millet, apple, parsley, marjoram, oregano, thyme, and black pepper. Add just enough broth to moisten and bind stuffing. Scoop insides from each tomato, leaving just a shell. Stuff each tomato two-thirds full.

Pour 1 cup water into pressure cooker and place trivet inside. Carefully arrange stuffed tomatoes on trivet, taking care that tomatoes do not touch the sides of cooker. Cover tomatoes to protect from condensation.

Seal cooker and bring to high pressure quickly. Lower heat and cook for 4 minutes. Reduce pressure quickly under cold running water, being careful not to slant cooker and topple the tomatoes. Gently remove tomatoes with tongs.

Stuffed Artichokes

Wash artichokes by plunging them top-first into a sink of water. Cut off the stems and remove the bottom leaves. Use kitchen scissors to trim ½ inch from the top of each artichoke; also cut off about one fourth of each leaf tip.

3	globe artichokes	½	cup diced tomato
1	tablespoon extra virgin olive oil	½	cup chopped fresh Italian parsley
½	cup minced yellow onion	2	tablespoons diced red bell pepper
1	clove garlic, minced		
1	cup diced zucchini	1	tablespoon balsamic vinegar

Special Equipment
Trivet, sprayed with vegetable oil

Pour 1 cup water into pressure cooker and place trivet inside. Place artichokes, stem ends down, on trivet. Seal cooker and bring to high pressure quickly. Lower heat and cook for 15 minutes. Reduce pressure quickly under cold running water.

Artichokes are done when a leaf near the center of each artichoke pulls out easily. If they are not completely cooked, reseal cooker, return to high pressure, lower heat, and cook for an additional 5 minutes. When artichokes are cooked, scrape out the fuzzy thistle center from each choke with a spoon and discard. Set artichokes aside to cool while preparing the sautéed vegetables.

Heat the olive oil in open pressure cooker over medium heat. Sauté onion and garlic until onion softens. Add zucchini, tomato, parsley, and red pepper and cook until tender. Thoroughly mix in the vinegar and fill the hollowed artichoke centers with sautéed vegetables.

Stuffings, Spreads, and Dips

Bean
Paté

MAKES ABOUT 1¼ CUPS

Serve with crackers or finger vegetables, such as carrots and mushrooms. Spread paté on bread for a sandwich filling.

1   cup cooked kidney beans
      (pages 28–29)

3   tablespoons smooth peanut
      butter

2   tablespoons tomato paste

Mash beans with fork and combine with peanut butter and tomato paste.

Hummus
(Chickpea Dip)

MAKES ABOUT 2¾ CUPS

Our favorite Middle Eastern dip. We like to serve hummus warm with the traditional drizzle of olive oil puddled on the top. Warm soft pita wedges for dipping complete this hearty lunch or snack. There are three ways of adding garlic to this recipe. For a tamer version, add the garlic while the chickpeas cook, or oven-roast a head of garlic and squeeze one or two cloves in with the chickpeas. For a livelier version, add the garlic raw. In any case, the more cloves the better.

2   cups well-cooked chickpeas
       (pages 28–29)
¼   cup freshly squeezed or frozen
       lemon juice
2   cloves garlic, minced

3   tablespoons tahini (sesame
       seed butter)
2   tablespoons extra virgin
       olive oil

Purée chickpeas, lemon juice, garlic, and ¼ cup water in food processor or blender. Add more water to get a creamy consistency. Transfer to a bowl and mix in tahini. Let sit for an hour to allow flavors to mingle. Drizzle olive oil over top and serve with warm pita bread wedges.

Fresh Herb Bean Spread

MAKES ABOUT 1¼ CUPS

With only three ingredients, this spread is easy and versatile. If you have an herb garden, throw in whatever is available. Season with salt, freshly ground black pepper, miso, or tamari.

1   cup well-cooked pinto beans (pages 28–29)

¼   cup nonfat yogurt

1   to 2 tablespoons chopped fresh herbs

Combine pinto beans, yogurt, and herbs in a food processor and blend until smooth. Use as a filling for sandwiches.

Sweet Potato Spread

MAKES 4 CUPS

Spread on whole grain bread for a real taste treat. Serve in a sandwich with fresh mozzarella and ripe tomato slices. A favorite with kids of any age.

4   cups peeled and cubed cooked sweet potatoes (pages 30–33)
1/2   cup potato cooking water
2   tablespoons tahini
1/4   teaspoon ground cinnamon

1/8   teaspoon salt
1   heaping tablespoon arrowroot powder dissolved in 2 tablespoons cold water

Purée sweet potatoes and cooking water in blender or food processor. Add this mixture and tahini, cinnamon, salt, and arrowroot slurry to empty cooker or another pan. Cook over medium-low heat until purée thickens, stirring constantly.

Chill in refrigerator and use as a spread. Add 1 tablespoon balsamic vinegar to mixture for a tangy, vibrant twist.

Polenta Taco Filling

SERVES 4

A great finger food for a Saturday lunch.

1	cup raw polenta	2	cups Vegetable Broth (page 108)
1	plum tomato, seeded and diced	4	blue-corn taco shells or tortillas
1	small hot green chile pepper, such as kenyan, minced	½	cup grated cheddar cheese
1	tablespoon ground cumin	½	cup chopped fresh cilantro
2	teaspoons chili powder	½	cup red onion, sliced thin
		½	cup salsa

Add polenta, tomato, chile pepper, cumin, chili powder, and broth to pressure cooker. Seal cooker and bring to high pressure quickly. Lower heat and cook for 5 minutes. Reduce pressure quickly under cold running water.

Fill taco shells with cheese, hot polenta, cilantro, red onion, and salsa. Serve.

Variation   *Add 1 cup cooked pinto beans to polenta mixture before cooking.*

Curried Lentil Spread

SERVES 4

A super-simple starter recipe. Wonderful spread on crackers and served with sliced tomatoes, eggplant, or red onions.

1 tablespoon curry powder

1 cup cooked red lentils
   (pages 28–29)

Mix curry powder and 2 tablespoons water into a paste. Mash lentils and curry together until well blended.

11

DESSERTS

Not only can the pressure cooker make hearty soups, flavorful salads, and great casseroles, it is also the perfect tool for making delicate custards and puddings. This chapter contains instructions for making such favorites as egg custard, bread pudding, fruit compote, and poached fresh fruit. General guidelines for making custards, bread puddings, and rice puddings, as well as timetables for dried and fresh fruit, can be found in chapter 3.

Warm comfort foods for unexpected guests or unexpected cravings can be made quickly with your pressure cooker. Foolproof desserts such as satiny custards are attainable with the constant heat of the pressure cooker. Use molds and glass and ceramic dishes inside your cooker, and serve the desserts directly from these dishes. If you don't already have cookware that fits into your pressure cooker, invest in some now.

Just remember, the thicker and heavier the ingredients, the longer they will take to cook. The test for doneness of steamed desserts is simple: Insert a knife into the center. If it comes out clean, then the dessert is done. If not, then seal the cooker and continue cooking for just a few more minutes.

DESSERT NUTRITION TIPS

- If calories are a concern, substitute lowfat or fat-free soymilk for regular soymilk.
- You can increase the fiber of these recipes by using whole grain breads and grains and sprinkling wheat germ on the top.
- Nuts are a great addition to many of these recipes but remember that each tablespoon of nuts is loaded with fat and calories. Nut oils are usually very heart-healthy but they can pad your waistline.

Honey Custard

An easy, basic recipe that can be modified to suit your needs and tastes. For a different taste, add 1 teaspoon coconut extract in place of the vanilla and garnish with toasted or dried shredded coconut.

2 cups milk of choice	1 teaspoon pure vanilla extract
3 eggs, slightly beaten	1/8 teaspoon salt
1/4 cup honey	Ground nutmeg for garnish

Special Equipment

Trivet
Four 6-ounce custard cups
Cover for cups (glass, wax paper, foil)

Pour 1 cup water into pressure cooker and place trivet inside. Coat custard cups with nonstick vegetable spray. In a small bowl beat together milk, eggs, honey, vanilla, and salt. Fill each custard cup two-thirds full. Cover securely and place on trivet.

Seal cooker and bring to high pressure slowly. Lower heat and cook for 4 minutes. Reduce pressure quickly under cold running water, being careful not to tilt cups.

Remove cups and chill in refrigerator. Sprinkle nutmeg on top before serving.

Bananas in Chocolate Custard

Yum, one of our favorite recipes! Use only high-quality cocoa and pure vanilla extract. For a plain egg custard, delete the cocoa and bananas and add 2 tablespoons sugar.

8	to 12 banana slices	$1/2$	cup premium sweetened cocoa
2	cups milk of choice	1	teaspoon pure vanilla extract
3	eggs, slightly beaten	$1/8$	teaspoon salt

Special Equipment

Trivet
Four 6-ounce custard cups
Cover for cups (glass, wax paper, foil)

Pour 1 cup water into pressure cooker and place trivet inside. Coat custard cups with nonstick vegetable spray. Place 2 or 3 banana slices in bottom of each cup.

In a small bowl beat together milk, eggs, cocoa, vanilla, and salt. Fill each custard cup two-thirds full. Cover securely and place on trivet.

Seal cooker and bring to high pressure slowly. Lower heat and cook for 4 minutes. Reduce pressure quickly under cold running water, being careful not to tilt cups.

Remove cups and chill in refrigerator. Invert each custard onto a plate so that banana slices are on top.

Grain Pudding

SERVES 4 TO 6

A great way to use up any leftover grains. The eggs can be omitted if you do not eat dairy products. If cholesterol is a concern, 2 egg whites can be substituted for each whole egg. We recommend raisins, dates, shredded coconut, and dried cranberries or cherries for the dried fruit, and honey, maple syrup, molasses, barley malt, or rice malt for the liquid sweetener.

2 cups milk of choice	¼ to ½ cup liquid sweetener of choice
1½ cups cooked grain of choice (pages 26–27)	½ teaspoon almond or pure vanilla extract
3 eggs, slightly beaten	
½ cup dried fruit of choice	

Special Equipment

Trivet

Glass ovenproof casserole that fits easily into your pressure cooker, with lid

Pour 1 cup water into pressure cooker and place trivet inside. Coat casserole dish with nonstick vegetable spray.

In a small bowl combine milk, grain, eggs, dried fruit, sweetener, and extract. Pour into prepared casserole. Do not fill dish over two-thirds full. Cover dish and place on trivet.

Seal cooker and bring to high pressure slowly. Lower heat and cook for 4 minutes. Reduce pressure quickly under cold running water, then remove dish. Serve warm or chilled.

Honey Rice Pudding

SERVES 4 TO 6

The ultimate comfort food. This recipe tastes especially good when made with regular soymilk.

2	cups milk of choice	⅓	cup honey
1½	cups cooked short grain brown rice (pages 26–27)	1	teaspoon pure vanilla extract
3	eggs, slightly beaten	½	teaspoon ground cinnamon
½	cup sultanas		Fruit for garnish

Special Equipment

Trivet

Glass ovenproof casserole that fits easily into your pressure cooker, with lid

Pour 1 cup water into pressure cooker and place trivet inside. Coat casserole dish with nonstick vegetable spray.

In a small bowl combine milk, rice, eggs, sultanas, honey, vanilla, and cinnamon. Pour into prepared casserole. Do not fill dish over two-thirds full. Cover dish and place on trivet.

Seal cooker and bring to high pressure slowly. Lower heat and cook for 4 minutes. Reduce pressure quickly under cold running water and remove dish. If desired, press rice into oiled mold and chill. Turn out onto plate and garnish with fruit.

Bread Pudding

SERVES 4

Any bread will work beautifully here—stale or fresh, whole wheat or mixed grain, crust on or off. A rich pudding can be made with whole eggs and whole milk, or a lean one with egg whites and skim milk.

For another variation, use almond or coconut extract in place of the vanilla. We recommend honey, molasses, maple syrup, or rice syrup for the liquid sweetener, and raisins, dates, dried cranberries, apricots, and chopped apple rings for the dried fruit.

2	cups milk of choice	1/4	cup dried fruit of choice
4	eggs, slightly beaten (or 2 eggs plus 4 egg whites)	2	teaspoons pure vanilla extract
1/2	cup liquid sweetener of choice	8	slices of bread
			Ground cinnamon

Special Equipment

Trivet

Glass ovenproof casserole that fits easily into your pressure cooker, with lid

Pour 1 cup water into pressure cooker and place trivet inside. Coat casserole dish with nonstick vegetable spray.

Combine milk, eggs, sweetener, dried fruit, and vanilla in bowl. Arrange 4 slices bread in prepared casserole dish and add half the milk mixture, making sure that all the bread is saturated. Repeat process with remaining bread and milk mixture. Cover dish securely and place on trivet.

Seal cooker and bring to high pressure slowly. Lower heat and cook for 15 minutes. Reduce pressure quickly under cold running water. Sprinkle with cinnamon and serve warm or chilled.

Desserts

Bread and Butter Pudding with Caramel Sauce

SERVES 4

We like to use extra-thick slices of fresh French bread for this pudding, but any kind of bread can be used. This is a rich version of bread pudding. It can be made leaner by substituting egg whites for some or all of the egg yolks, substituting skim milk for whole, and omitting the butter.

6	tablespoons dark brown sugar	2	teaspoons pure vanilla extract
2	cups whole milk of choice	1	teaspoon ground cinnamon
4	eggs, slightly beaten	8	slices bread, buttered
1/2	cup honey	1/4	cup sultanas

Special Equipment

Trivet
Four 10-ounce custard cups
Cover for cups (glass, wax paper, foil)

Pour 1 cup water into pressure cooker and place trivet inside. Coat custard cups with nonstick vegetable spray. Press 1 1/2 tablespoons of brown sugar into the bottom of each cup.

Mix milk, eggs, honey, vanilla, and cinnamon together in a bowl. Place 1 slice buttered bread in each cup, and pour half the milk mixture into the 4 cups. Sprinkle half the sultanas over the bread and milk mixture. Repeat process with remaining bread, milk mixture, and sultanas. Cover custard cups securely and place on trivet.

Seal cooker and bring to high pressure slowly. Lower heat and cook for 15 minutes. Reduce pressure quickly under cold running water. Remove cups from cooker and let sit until warm or chill in refrigerator. Unmold, allowing sugar sauce to flow down sides of pudding.

Rum-Stewed Fruit

SERVES 4

This recipe makes a great topping for ice cream, yogurt, pancakes, and waffles. The small bit of rum in this recipe will not cook away, so substitute 1 teaspoon rum extract if you want to avoid alcohol. Do not fill the cooker over half full. The cooking fruit needs room to expand.

2	cups apple juice	1/3	cup dried apple rings, snipped into 1/2-inch pieces
1/3	cup dried cranberries		
1/3	cup dried golden sultanas	2	to 4 tablespoons rum
		1/2	teaspoon ground allspice

Add to pressure cooker apple juice, cranberries, sultanas, dried apple, rum, and allspice. Seal cooker and bring to high pressure slowly. Lower heat and cook for 5 minutes. Reduce pressure quickly under cold running water. Spoon over dessert or breakfast of choice.

Gingered Fruit Bowl

A very easy dessert. The dried fruit can be stored in your pantry until needed. Lemon adds a high note to the sweetness of this compote. We recommend apples, apricots, pears, and prunes for the dried fruit, and grapes, cherries, and oranges for the fresh fruit.

1   cup mixed dried fruit of choice
1/3 cup mixed fresh fruit of choice
2   teaspoons grated fresh ginger
      or 1/4 teaspoon ground

1   teaspoon freshly grated or
      dried lemon zest
1   teaspoon freshly squeezed
      lemon juice
1   cinnamon stick, 6 inches long

Add to pressure cooker dried fruit, fresh fruit, ginger, lemon zest, lemon juice, and cinnamon stick. Seal cooker and bring to high pressure slowly. Lower heat and cook for 10 minutes. Reduce pressure quickly under cold running water.

Remove cinnamon stick. Top compote with custard, vanilla yogurt, or cream, or spoon it over yogurt, ice cream, cereal, custard, or pancakes.

Stuffed Apples

Be careful not to cook the apples too long or they will turn into apple-sauce. For a festive flair, drizzle melted chocolate over the apples instead of honey.

4   large cooking apples, cored   Honey to taste
1   cup granola

Special Equipment
Trivet
Four 6-ounce custard cups
Cover for cups (glass, wax paper, foil)

Pour 1 cup water into pressure cooker and place trivet inside. Place 1 apple in each custard cup and press granola into hollow core. Cover cups securely and lay on trivet.

Seal cooker and bring to high pressure quickly. Lower heat and cook for 5 minutes. Reduce pressure quickly under cold running water.

Sprinkle tops of apples with any remaining granola, drizzle with honey, and serve warm.

Spice House Pears

Pears take well to poaching. They hold their shape and even grainy pulp turns smooth. If you are using underripe hard pears, add 1 minute to the cooking time. If your pears are a bit overripe, decrease cooking time by 1 minute. Star anise is beautiful and fragrant. It can be found at gourmet shops and often in the bulk spices section of your local grocery store.

1	cup dry white wine	1	teaspoon lemon zest
3	stars anise	4	Comice pears, cored
1	vanilla bean	1/4	teaspoon saffron threads
2	cinnamon sticks, 5 inches long each	1/2	cup honey

Add wine, anise, vanilla bean, cinnamon sticks, and lemon zest to pressure cooker. Stand pears in cooking liquid, being careful not to let the pears touch the sides of the cooker.

Seal cooker and bring to high pressure slowly. Lower heat and cook for 8 minutes. Reduce pressure quickly under cold running water.

Transfer pears to small custard cups and crumble saffron on top. Remove anise, vanilla bean, and cinnamon sticks from cooking liquid. Add honey and simmer in open cooker until liquid is reduced to a glaze. Spoon glaze generously over pears.

Poppy Seed Pudding

SERVES 4 TO 6

Experiment with different types of flour. Brown rice flour can be used for celiacs, spelt flour for those allergic to common wheat. Texture and nutritional value will be lost if you use white flour. We recommend walnuts, almonds, or cashews for the crushed nuts.

²/₃	cup poppy seeds	¹/₂	cup molasses
²/₃	cup finely crushed nuts	¹/₂	cup boiling water
¹/₄	cup raisins	2¹/₂	cups flour of choice
¹/₂	teaspoon ground ginger	1	teaspoon baking soda
1	egg, slightly beaten	¹/₂	teaspoon salt
¹/₂	cup honey		

Special Equipment

Trivet
Well-oiled pudding mold that fits easily into your pressure cooker

Pour 2 cups water into pressure cooker and place trivet inside. In a large bowl, combine poppy seeds, nuts, raisins, and ginger. Mix in beaten egg, honey, molasses, and boiling water, stirring well after each addition.

In a separate bowl, combine flour, baking soda, and salt. Add flour mixture to wet ingredients and gently mix. Pour immediately into mold, filling no more than two-thirds full. Set filled mold on trivet.

Seal cooker but remove pressure regulator. Cook for 15 minutes on high heat without pressure. Water can steam away very quickly when the pressure regulator is not used. Watch the water level: steam should escape in a steady stream. If it slows down or stops, you're out of water and need to add more.

Replace pressure regulator and bring to high pressure quickly. Cook for 15 more minutes at high pressure. Let pressure fall slowly on its own. Unmold immediately and serve warm or cold.

Almond Pudding

This is a steamed pudding, which is quite different than creamy puddings. Steamed puddings traditionally require 2 to 3 hours of slow cooking, making them good candidates for pressure cooking. With the pressure cooker, the puddings are cooked for the first 15 minutes without pressure to allow the leavened batter to rise.

Cook these recipes in molds if at all possible. They make lovely desserts for company.

1	egg, slightly beaten	1¾	cups whole grain flour of choice
½	cup molasses	3	tablespoons butter, room temperature
½	cup hot water		
1	to 2 tablespoons almond extract	1	cup chopped pitted prunes
½	teaspoon baking soda	½	cup ground almonds

Special Equipment
Trivet
Well-oiled pudding mold that fits easily into your pressure cooker

Pour 2 cups water into pressure cooker and place trivet inside. In a large bowl whisk together egg, molasses, water, almond extract, and baking soda. Mix in flour, butter, prunes, and almonds, stirring well after each addition. Pour immediately into mold, filling no more than two-thirds full.

Set filled mold on trivet. Seal cooker but remove pressure regulator. Cook for 15 minutes on high heat without pressure. Water can steam away very quickly when the pressure regulator is not used.

Steam should escape in a steady stream. If it slows down or stops, you're out of water and need to add more.

Replace pressure regulator and bring to high pressure quickly. Cook for 15 more minutes at high pressure. Let pressure fall slowly on its own. Unmold immediately and serve warm or cold.

Chocolate Steamed Pudding

SERVES 6

A real treat for all those chocoholics out there. This steamed pudding is a nice change-of-pace from creamy-type puddings. We love this served warm with a bit of whipped cream or bananas on top. Or serve it spooned into dessert dishes topped with a cherry sauce.

½	cup honey	¼	cup premium sweetened cocoa
3	tablespoons butter, melted	2	teaspoons baking powder
1	egg, slightly beaten	¼	teaspoon salt
2	teaspoons pure vanilla extract	1	cup milk of choice
2¼	cups whole grain flour of choice		

Special Equipment

Trivet
Well-oiled pudding mold that fits easily into your pressure cooker

Pour 2 cups water into pressure cooker and place trivet inside. In a large bowl whisk honey, melted butter, egg, and vanilla. Sift together flour, cocoa, baking powder, and salt. Alternately add dry ingredients and milk to the honey mixture, stirring well after each addition, until all is combined. Pour immediately into mold, filling no more than two-thirds full.

Set filled mold on trivet. Seal cooker but remove pressure regulator. Cook for 15 minutes on high heat without pressure. Water can steam away very quickly when the pressure regulator is not used.

Steam should escape in a steady stream. If it slows down or stops, you're out of water and need to add more.

Replace pressure regulator and bring to high pressure quickly. Cook for 15 more minutes at high pressure. Let pressure fall slowly on its own. Unmold immediately and serve warm or cold.

Berry Bananas

SERVES 2

You can use either fresh or frozen raspberries in this recipe. Strawberries also work well. The berries can be added before or after cooking.

2   ripe bananas, peeled   ½   cup raspberries

Special Equipment
Trivet
Oval baking dish that fits easily into your cooker, with lid

Pour 1 cup water into pressure cooker and place trivet inside. Place whole bananas in baking dish, sprinkle berries on top, cover, and place on trivet.

Seal cooker and bring to high pressure quickly. Lower heat and cook for 6 minutes. Reduce pressure quickly under cold running water. Serve warm in banana-split boats.

Mail-Order Sources

If you can't get out of the house to buy some of the ingredients used in this book or if you cannot find them locally, try these mail-order companies.

Arrowhead Mills
110 South Lawton
Hereford, TX 79045
(806) 364-0730
1-800-749-0730

Call for a free catalog. This quality company carries ancient whole grains and products such as amaranth, quinoa, kamut flour, and spelt flour in bulk.

Bob's Red Mill
Natural Foods, Inc.
5209 SE International Way
Milwaukee, OR 97222
(503) 654-3215
1-800-553-2258

This company sells whole grain products including ancient grains such as teff, spelt, and quinoa. They also have an extensive catalog boasting such quality products as whole amaranth, hulled barley, and buckwheat groats. They carry many hard-to-find products and have an outstanding customer service department.

Deer Valley Farm
PO Box 173
Guilford, NY 13780-0173
(607) 764-8556

Call for a free catalog. This company carries grains and seeds such as kamut, spelt, and quinoa.

Niblack Foods, Inc.
900 Jefferson Road, Bldg. #5
Rochester, NY 14623
(716) 292-0790
1-800-724-8883

Send for a price list. This company carries whole grain flours as well as whole grains such as quinoa, amaranth, spelt, and kamut. They supply commercial bakers and can handle orders of large quantities.

Sam Wylde
PO Box 84488
Seattle, WA 98124
(206) 762-5400
1-800-325-9788

Call for a free catalog. This is the parent company for Ener-G Foods (manufacturers of high-quality whole grain baking products). They carry grain products such as wheat berries, cracked rye, cornmeal, and millet.

Walnut Acres
Penns Creek, PA 17862
1-800-433-3998

Call for a free catalog and ask for the "No-room-in-the-catalog" sheet that lists many of the more unusual whole grains that have been special customer requests. They have an impressive product list of baking goods and packaged health foods such as nut butters, dried fruits, and soups.

Glossary

allspice   This mildly sharp spice is made of the berry of the West Indian allspice tree. Its scent resembles a combination of cloves, cinnamon, and nutmeg. Widely available in grocery stores and gourmet shops.

amaranth   Amaranth seeds have a sweet nutty flavor that makes the flour ideal for baking cookies and pastries. For a morning burst, cook it into a hot cereal. Amaranth is high in protein, fiber, calcium, iron, and vitamin C. The seeds can be purchased at health food and gourmet stores, through mail-order sources, and at most supermarkets.

Anaheim chile pepper   (also New Mexico pepper, Rio Grande pepper, and California pepper) A richer source of vitamin C than citrus fruits, this pepper contains as much beta-carotene as a carrot does. Found fresh in the produce section of most grocery stores.

balsamic vinegar   Made from white grapes, balsamic vinegar is aged for several years in wood barrels. The vinegar is dark brown, with a mellow sweet-and-sour flavor. Found in the gourmet section or near salad dressings in grocery stores.

barley   The whole barley grain has a sweet flavor and resilient texture. The tough outer layer of barley is removed and the grain is polished. When the grain has been highly refined through a process of five or six polishings, it has lost its hull, bran, and most of its germ, and is then known as pearled barley. Whole unpearled barley is nutritionally valuable and is an excellent source of starch as well as potassium, magnesium, and niacin. Can be purchased in bulk or in bags at grocery stores.

blue corn Corn grows in a rainbow of colors. White and yellow are the most common in North America but recently blue corn has made a comeback. Blue corn is higher in protein than its counterparts. Available fresh-frozen at most grocery stores.

bok choy (also Chinese cabbage, pak choy, and pak choi) With long white ribs and elongated dark green leaves, this vegetable resembles chard. Bok choy supplies vitamin C and beta-carotene. Available in the produce section of many grocery stores and farmers markets.

bulgur A staple grain in southeastern Europe and the Middle East, bulgur is cracked wheat that has been lightly toasted. Available in bulk or boxed in many grocery stores. Can also be purchased through mail order and in gourmet shops.

cannellini beans This Argentinean bean is now closely associated with Italian cooking and is grown primarily in Italy. These oval white beans are smooth in texture and have a subtly nutty flavor. They are now widely available in grocery stores.

capers Grown in mountainous regions of Africa, Italy, France, and Spain. These small unopened flower buds of a Mediterranean bush add a briny, pungent flavor to dishes. Available in gourmet sections of the grocery store.

cardamom Cardamom has a eucalyptus-like scent and flavor common to East Indian cuisine. The pods can be purchased whole, and powdered cardamom is available at health food, specialty, and grocery stores, and through most spice companies.

chipatis This freckled flat bread is similar to the tortilla. Chipatis is an Indian staple made from whole wheat flour, salt, water, and small amounts of oil cooked in a heavy skillet, griddle, or wood-burning stove. The bread can be purchased at health food and grocery stores.

cinnamon This spice is actually the dried bark of an evergreen tree. American bakers use imported cinnamon from Indonesia and China. It is dark reddish-brown and has a warm, sweet flavor. Available ground in most groceries and in gourmet shops in sticks of rolled bark.

coconut milk and coconut cream Originally canned for Asian and Latin supermarkets, these products are now widely available in stores across the country. Many people have discovered the creamy, rich texture and sweet flavor that coconut milk imparts to soups, stews, beverages, puddings, rice dishes, and sauces. Now available in reduced-fat form. Find in ethnic sections of the grocery store, health food and gourmet shops.

coriander seed These aromatic seeds come from the pungent herb also known as Chinese parsley or cilantro. Coriander seed is often ground and used commercially in curry powders and pickling spice mixtures. You will find ground coriander in most grocery stores and as whole seeds in gourmet and health food shops.

cumin From Iran and Morocco, this aromatic seed has an earthy taste we associate with southwestern dishes in the U.S. This savory spice is best freshly ground in a coffee grinder or with pestle and mortar. Whole seeds can be purchased at gourmet shops and powdered form is widely available at grocery stores.

currants Native to Scandinavia and now widely cultivated in North America, these berries are dried and used like raisins. They may be red, white, or black, fresh or dried. Zante currants are actually dried grapes and can be found in gourmet shops in bulk or packed in boxes.

date sugar Crystallized, dried date powder is a terrific sweetener. Its rich flavor adds depth to recipes that refined, bleached white sugar does not. Date sugar is also a more nutritious sweetener than white sugar, as it is rich in potassium, calcium, and magnesium.

dill Grown primarily in California, this tangy herb has small tan seeds and feathery leaves. The whole seeds are sometimes ground and the leaves used fresh or dried. Available in most groceries.

dry mustard Grown in Asia, these tiny white, yellow, and brown seeds are ground for use in prepared mustards, used as a dip, and roasted whole to add a tangy bite to many dishes. Available in the spice section of most groceries.

fennel Fennel is a celery-like shoot with feathery leaves and a delicate aniseed flavor. It can be used cooked or raw. Serve a bowl of bite-sized pieces as an after-dinner digestive aid and breath freshener. Fennel can be purchased fresh in the produce section of most grocery stores.

garlic A single head of garlic contains many small cloves. Garlic has a pungent aroma and strong zesty flavor. Garlic contains an aromatic oil called allicin which has strong medicinal properties as a natural antibiotic.

ginger Grown in southern Asia, West Indies, and Africa. This light brown root has a peppery, spicy flavor. It can be purchased as fresh root, dried, candied (crystallized), and ground as a powder. Fresh ginger can be steeped in water to make a spicy digestive aid tea. Ginger is used in sweet as well as savory dishes and everything from pastries to fish dishes.

horseradish root A native to Eastern Europe and cultivated today in the United States, this pungent cylindrical root can be purchased fresh in the produce section of the market, grated and packed in jars, and dried or powdered and sold in the spice section of most grocery stores.

hot chile pepper   Capsaicin is the compound found in the seeds and veins but not in the walls of peppers. It is this compound that gives peppers their fiery heat. Chiles range on the heat index from mild peperoncinis to incendiary Tabasco. They can purchased fresh in the produce departments of most grocery stores, or dried and sold as flakes in the spice section of groceries and gourmet shops.

Italian parsley   The flat-leaf Italian variety of parsley is more pungent than its curly counterpart. It is also softer and easier to chew. Adding fresh Italian parsley leaves to salads, soups, and dressings will bring a fresh, bright flavor to the dish.

Jerusalem artichoke   This potato-like tuber has a distinctive flavor reminiscent of the globe artichoke. It can be mashed, puréed, or eaten whole just like a potato. Jerusalem artichokes are available in most grocery store produce sections.

kamut   Whole kamut kernels resemble large, golden grains of rice with a distinguishing hump. They have a rich buttery flavor and chewy texture. A rich source of protein, magnesium, and potassium, kamut is a good substitute for brown rice. The kernels can be purchased in bulk or packaged, and kamut flour is now widely available.

kohlrabi   The Germans named this vegetable "cabbage-turnip"; it is reminiscent of both in taste and appearance. The green- or purple-skinned Northern European vegetable is becoming popular in North America. Kohlrabi bulbs contain vitamin C and calcium. It can be purchased fresh in the produce section of the grocery store, and will keep in the refrigerator for up to a week.

kombu   Kombu is a sea vegetable eaten cooked or raw. Its salty robust flavor and mineral-rich content make it a popular addition to many dishes. It can be purchased raw or dried and added before cooking to infuse other foods in a recipe. It is available at health food, specialty, and grocery stores, Asian markets, and through mail order.

millet   This small, yellow, beadlike grain has a mild nutty flavor and fluffy texture. Millet is a high-protein grain. Its seeds are available in bulk or packaged in grocery stores.

mint   Commonly grown in Belgium, France, and Germany, this dark-emerald herb can be found fresh, dried, ground, or as an oil extract. It imparts a menthol flavor when added to bean and fish dishes, teas and salads. Mint can easily be grown on a windowsill, purchased at markets, or ordered through the mail.

mirin This sweet rice cooking wine is traditionally used in sauces and marinades, or mixed with sushi rice to add sweetness and stickiness for rice balls and sushi. Mirin is available at health food and grocery stores, and in Asian markets.

miso Miso is a fermented soybean paste combined with rice or barley, commonly used as a concentrated flavoring for gravies, salad dressings, sauces, marinades, and stews. It is also used as soup base. Miso colors range from red to brown to white, and its flavors range from strong and pungent to sweet and light. It is available in Asian markets and in grocery stores.

nutmeg Originally from Java, Malaya, and Granada, this mellow, nutty spice is ground and added to puddings, quiches, vegetables dishes, dressings, and sauces. Nutmeg is sold primarily in ground form in the spice section of the grocery store. But true nutmeg connoisseurs always buy whole nutmeg berries and grate them for the freshest, most pungent flavor.

olive oil, extra virgin This popular Mediterranean oil is the result of the first cold pressing of harvested olives. Subsequent pressings use heat and produce a lower-quality oil. Always use extra virgin olive oil in cooking.

oyster mushroom This exotic mushroom is grown in North America, Europe, and Asia. Oyster mushrooms are a beige-cream color and have a melting texture. They can be purchased dried or fresh in grocery stores, Asian markets, and specialty stores.

paprika Grown in Central America, southern Europe, and California, paprika is actually a mild capsicum. This slightly piquant spice adds mild flavor and color to warm dishes, soups, and beverages. Sold dried and powdered in the spice section of the grocery store.

Parmesan cheese This raw-milk, unpasteurized cheese is aged at least 60 days and has a strong flavor. It is also high in sodium. Use a small amount of this cheese to flavor grain and beans dishes or to top salads and soups.

parsley This curly herb has a sweet, fresh flavor. It can be purchased fresh and as dried flakes. Often eaten fresh after meals as a digestive aid and breath freshener. May be eaten before meals as an appetite stimulant.

parsnip This sweet root vegetable is a member of the carrot family, but it must be cooked. Can be found in most grocery store produce departments.

polenta This thick Italian porridge is made with coarsely ground cornmeal. Use plain cooked polenta as an alternative to rice to serve with cooked vegetables and beans. Available in grocery stores packaged as polenta or cornmeal.

quinoa Originally from South America, and pronounced *keen-wa*, this tiny, delicate, fluffy grain is rich in protein, vitamin E, riboflavin, and carotenes. It can be purchased in health food, gourmet, and grocery stores. Many mail-order catalogs also carry quinoa.

rutabaga Rutabagas are root vegetables with slightly sweet flavor. They can be eaten raw or cooked, and are delicious combined with other root vegetables. Look for rutabagas in the produce section of most grocery stores.

saffron This valuable spice is grown in Spain. Its delicate orange filaments impart a bright yellow color to dishes and a pleasantly bitter flavor. Used traditionally in arroz con pollo, paella, curried dishes, and bouillabaisse. Saffron is expensive if purchased in jars but can be very inexpensive if purchased in the bulk foods department of gourmet shops or grocery stores. Ask for it if you can't find it.

savory This aromatic herb can be used as whole dried leaves or ground in stews, chowders, and salad dressings. Available in grocery stores and gourmet shops.

sesame oil Usually associated with Asian cooking, this nutty-flavored oil, high in polyunsaturated fats, can be used sparingly to add tremendous flavor to grain dishes, vegetable sautés, and Asian bean dishes. Also available in flavors such as toasted sesame oil or hot chile pepper sesame oil.

sherry This fortified, amber-colored wine of southern Spain is usually inexpensive, and ranges from the very dry to the very sweet. It adds depth of flavor to soups, stews, salad dressings, and rich desserts. Available at most grocery stores.

shiitake mushroom This Asian mushroom has a cream-colored interior and a supple-firm texture. Shiitake mushrooms can often be purchased fresh in the produce department of grocery or gourmet stores. Available through mail-order catalogs and Asian markets, dried or fresh.

soy sauce Add a splash of this popular salty Asian condiment to cooked grain, vegetable, and bean dishes. Available in most grocery stores in the ethnic food section, in gourmet shops, and Asian markets.

spelt The cooked kernels of this nutritious whole grain are sweet and nutty, with a rice-like texture. Spelt is an excellent source of protein, magnesium, zinc, copper, and iron. Look for it in health food stores, grocery stores, and through mail-order sources.

star anise The whole anise pod is shaped like a beautiful star. Whole pods can steep in soups and sauces and are easily removed. Out of the pod, the individual seeds can be used whole or ground. Ground anise powder is commonly available in the spice department of grocery stores.

sun-dried tomato   Available jarred in olive oil or dried, sun-dried tomatoes are rich in flavor and a little goes a long way. Oil-soaked tomatoes are high in fat but their dried counterpart is virtually fat-free and can be reconstituted in hot water before cooking. You will find them in health food and grocery stores, and in gourmet markets.

sweet potato   Two varieties of sweet potato are the most common in the United States: One has a yellow flesh and a dry texture, the other has a sweet orange flesh and a watery texture (often incorrectly called yams). The two types can be used interchangeably in recipes, or cooked as you would white potatoes—mashed, baked or puréed. Sweet potatoes are a rich source of carotene and vitamin C. They are available in the produce section of the grocery store.

tamari   The wheat-free version of soy sauce has been used for centuries in China and Japan. This fermented soy product is stronger and sweeter in flavor than soy sauce, but they can be used interchangeably in recipes. Tamari is available in most grocery stores in the ethnic food section and in gourmet shops and Asian markets.

teff   This tiny dark brown grain has a nutty, sweet flavor. It is delicious as a base for vegetable dishes. When cooked, teff resembles caviar and its texture lends itself well to dips and cold salads.

tempeh   High in protein and a good source of B vitamins, tempeh is a fermented soybean product that can be used as a meat alternative. It is available in health food stores, Asian markets, many grocery stores, and through mail-order sources.

tofu   Also known as soybean curd, tofu is very adaptable and user-friendly. Now available fresh packed in water and packaged in plastic tubs. Also sold nationwide in aseptic packages which have a long shelf life and do not need to be refrigerated. The fresh variety is available with fiber and is best as a meat or egg alternative. The packaged variety is available in smooth, firm, and/or soft textures. They have reduced fiber and are best as a base for puddings, pie fillings, and casseroles. Many brands are also available in full-fat or reduced-fat.

turmeric   Grown in India this yellow-orange root is ground and used to add color and a musky and slightly bitter taste to such dishes as tofu, curries, rice, soups, and egg dishes as well as relishes and sauces. In India turmeric has long been used topically as a natural antibiotic and internally to help stave off bacterial and viral infection. Available ground in the spice department of grocery stores and as a paste in specialty shops.

yam This woody tuber has brown skin and sweet moist flesh. Yams can be cooked as you would sweet potatoes or white potatoes. They are available in the produce section of most grocery stores.

Index

Index

Index

T